# Task-Focused Summarization and Question Answering Workshop 2006



**Held in conjunction with COLING/ACL 2006**

## Sydney, Australia
## 23 July 2006

ISBN: 978-1-61738-508-7

**Printed from e-media with permission by:**

Curran Associates, Inc.
57 Morehouse Lane
Red Hook, NY 12571
www.proceedings.com

**Some format issues inherent in the e-media version may also appear in this print version.**



Printed by Curran Associates, Inc. (2010)



Association for Computational Linguistics
209 N. Eighth Street
Stroudsburg, Pennsylvania 18360

Phone: 1-570-476-8006
Fax: 1-570-476-0860

acl@aclweb.org

# Table of Contents

# Preface

The *Task-Focused Summarization and Question Answering* workshop, to be held on July 23, 2006 in Sydney, aims to bring together the two communities of summarization and question answering by examining how to create output that is directed to a user's needs, i.e., how to create task-focused output. The user scenarios that are described in the accepted papers include the medical and computer domain, readers of short stories and also traditional multidocument news collections, some with interesting, and different, evaluation methodologies. By focusing on the benefits that summarization and question answering can have for users, we hope to contribute to the discussion of the evaluation in both areas.

We included the call for papers in these proceedings. Of the fourteen papers submitted, we accepted seven to be presented at the workshop. We want to thank all the members of the program committee for their thoughtful and in depth reviews. All the reviews were completed on time, despite very tight deadlines.

We wanted to invite a speaker who is deeply involved in both the question answering and summarization communities and who can help bring the communities further together. We thank Sanda Harabagiu for her talk, as well as for her support in this area. Furthermore, we hope that convening a panel to bring together researchers engaged in evaluation of summarization and question answering from around the world will increase our understanding of the current state of the art in evaluation and provide opportunties to share our understanding.

Finally, we thank the workshop participants for sharing their current work at this workshop, and for sharing with us their views on the utility of summarization and question answering to users' needs.

Tat-Seng Chua, Jade Goldstein, Simone Teufel, Lucy Vanderwende

# Excerpts from Call for Papers

This one-day workshop will focus on the challenges that the Summarization and QA communities face in developing useful systems and in developing evaluation measures. Our aim is to bring these two communities together to discuss the current challenges and to learn from each other's approaches, following the success of a similar workshop held at ACL-05, which brought together the Machine Translation and Summarization communities.

A previous summarization workshop (*Text Summarization Branches Out*, ACL-04) targeted the exploration of different scenarios for summarization, such as small mobile devices, legal texts, speech, dialog, email and other genres. We encourage a deeper analysis of these, and other, user scenarios, focusing on the utility of summarization and question answering for such scenarios and genres, including cross-lingual ones.

By focusing on the measurable benefits that summarization and question answering has for users, we hope one of the outcomes of this workshop will be to better motivate research and focus areas for summarization and question answering, and to establish task-appropriate evaluation methods. Given a user scenario, it would ideally be possible to demonstrate that a given evaluation method predicts greater/lesser utility for users. We especially encourage papers describing intrinsic and extrinsic evaluation metrics in the context of these user scenarios.

Both summarization and QA have a long history of evaluations: Summarization since 1998 (SUMMAC) and QA since 1999 (TREC). The importance of summarization evaluation is evidenced by the many DUC workshops; in DUC-05, extensive discussions were held regarding the use of ROUGE, ROUGE-BE, and the pyramid method, a semantic-unit based approach, for evaluating summarization systems. The QA community has related evaluation issues for answers to complex questions such as the TREC definition questions. Some common considerations in both communities include what constitutes a good answer/response to an information request, and how does one determine whether a "complex" answer is sufficient? In both communities, as well as in the distillation component of the 2005 DARPA program GALE, researchers are exploring how to capture semantic equivalence among components of different answers (nuggets, factoids or SCUs). There also have been efforts to design new automatic scoring measures, such as ROUGE-BE and POURPRE. We encourage papers discussing these and other metrics that report on how well the metric correlates with human judgments and/or predicts effectiveness in task-focused scenarios for summarization and QA.

This workshop is a continuation of ACL 2005 for the summarization community, In which those interested in evaluation measures participated in a joint Workshop on evaluation for summarization and MT. As a sequel to the ACL 2005 workshop, in which the results of the first Multilingual multidocument summarization evaluation (MSE) were presented, we plan to report and discuss the results of the 2006 MSE evaluation.

In summary, we solicit papers on any or all of the following three topics:

- Task-based user scenarios requiring question answering (beyond factoids/lists) and/or summarization, across genres and languages
- Extrinsic and intrinsic evaluations, correlating extrinsic measures with outcome of task completion and/or intrinsic measures with human judgments previously obtained.
- The 2006 Multilingual Multidocument Summarization Evaluation

Anyone with an interest in summarization, QA and/or evaluation is encouraged to participate in the workshop. We are looking for research papers in the aforementioned topics, as well as position papers that identify limitations in current approaches and describe promising future research directions.

# Multilingual Summarization Evaluation 2006

The 2nd Multilingual Summarization Evaluation will be held in conjunction with the COLING//ACL 2006 Workshop *Task-Focused Summarization and Question Answering* and the results of the evaluation will be reported during the COLING/ACL Workshop. This evaluation repeats the first Multilingual Summarization Evaluation held in 2005 as part of the ACL workshop *Intrinsic and Extrinsic Evaluation Measures for MT and/or Summarization.*

Task Description:

Given a cluster of documents on the same event, some in English, some translated from Arabic (Arabic source is also available), generate a 100-word summary of the event. Clusters contain on average 10 documents per cluster. The distribution between Arabic and English varies between clusters.

Data:

25 clusters from the Multilingual Summarziation Evaluation 2005 are available for training, as well as the DUC2004 data for Task 4, available at http://duc.nist.gov.

25 clusters will be used for testing. These clusters were created by running a clustering algorithm developed by Columbia over the the TDT4 corpus, which contains 41,728 Arabic documents and 23,602 English documents. ISI's MT system was used to translate the Arabic data. Both source and translation are available in the cluster. Human annotators at the LDC sorted through the automatically created clusters, to select 50 (25 clusters for last year, 25 clusters for this year) that were good to use, editing the clusters as needed. Four humans wrote a 100-word summary for each cluster. Thus, there are 4 model summaries per cluster.

Organizers:

Jade Goldstein, US Department of Defense
Lucy Vanderwende, Microsoft Research
Liang Zhou, USC/ISI

Participants:

Lehmam Abderrafih, Pertinence Mining
John M. Conroy, Dianne P. O'Leary, Judith D. Schlesinger, IDA/CCS and University of Maryland Angelo Dalli, University of Sheffield
David Kirk Evans, Japanese National Institute of Information
Maher Jaoua, MIRACL Laboratory for Computer Sciences, University of Sfax, Tunisia
Wenjie Li, Department of Computing, The Hong Kong Polytechnic University
Prasad Pingali, Jagadeesh J, Vasudeva Varma, IIIT, Hyderabad
Wei Xu, Tsinghua University, Beijing, China
David Zajic, University of Maryland and BBN Technologies (UMD/BBN)

# Organizers

**Chairs:**

Tat-Seng Chua, National University of Singapore (Singapore)
Jade Goldstein, US Department of Defense (USA)
Simone Teufel, Cambridge University (UK)
Lucy Vanderwende, Microsoft Research (USA)

**Program Committee:**

Regina Barzilay, MIT (USA)
Sabine Bergler, Concordia University (Canada)
Silviu Cucerzan, Microsoft Research (USA)
Hang Cui, National University of Singapore (Singapore)
Krzysztof Czuba, Google (USA)
Hal Daume III, USC/ISI (USA)
Hans van Halteren, Radboud University, Nijmegen (Netherlands)
Sanda Harabagiu, University of Texas, Dallas (USA)
Chiori Hori, Carnegie Mellon University (USA)
Eduard Hovy, USC/ISI (USA)
Hongyan Jing, IBM Research (USA)
Guy Lapalme, University of Montreal (Canada)
Geunbae (Gary) Lee, Postech Univ (Korea)
Chin-Yew Lin, Microsoft Research Asia (China)
Inderjeet Mani, MITRE (USA)
Marie-France Moens, Katholieke Universiteit Leuven (Belgium)
Ani Nenkova, Columbia University (USA)
Manabu Okumura, Tokyo Institute of Technology (Japan)
John Prager, IBM Research (USA)
Horacio Saggion, University of Sheffield (UK)
Judith Schlesinger, IDA/CCS (USA)
Karen Sparck Jones, University of Cambridge (UK)
Nicola Stokes, University of Melbourne (Australia)
Beth Sundheim, SPAWAR Systems Center (USA)
Tomek Strzalkowski, University at Albany (USA)
Ralph Weischedel, BBN (USA)

**Invited Speaker:**

Sanda Harabagiu, Language Computer Corporation (USA)

**Panelists:**

Hoa Trang Dang, NIST (USA)
Eduard Hovy, USC/ISI (USA)
Noriko Kando, NTCIR (Japan)

# Scenario Based Question Answering

**Sanda Harabagiu**

When faced with a task described by a complex scenario, users ask questions that are motivated by the need to explore complex relationships. These questions test the capabilities of Q/A systems to (1) tackle complex requests; (2) take into account the scenario context; and (3) enable a coherent dialogue with the user.

In this talk I shall describe our experience with Ferret, our interactive Q/A system, within several experiments that involved multiple scenarios and a varied number of users. I shall present the lessons learned and focus on the most challenging problems.

# Workshop Program

**Sunday, 23 July 2006**

| | |
|---|---|
| 8:30–8:40 | Opening Remarks |
| | **Session 1: Summarization** |
| 8:40–9:05 | *Dimensionality Reduction Aids Term Co-Occurrence Based Multi-Document Summarization* |
| | Ben Hachey, Gabriel Murray and David Reitter |
| 9:05–9:30 | *Challenges in Evaluating Summaries of Short Stories* |
| | Anna Kazantseva and Stan Szpakowicz |
| | **Session 2: Invited Talk** |
| 9:30–10:30 | Invited Talk, *Scenario-based Question Answering* by Sanda Harabagiu |
| 10:30-10:50 | Break |
| | **Session 3: Question Answering** |
| 10:50–11:15 | *Question Pre-Processing in a QA System on Internet Discussion Groups* |
| | Chuan-Jie Lin and Chun-Hung Cho |
| 11:15–11:40 | *Situated Question Answering in the Clinical Domain: Selecting the Best Drug Treatment for Diseases* |
| | Dina Demner-Fushman and Jimmy Lin |
| 11:40–12:05 | *Using Scenario Knowledge in Automatic Question Answering* |
| | Sanda Harabagiu and Andrew Hickl |
| 12:05–12:30 | *Automating Help-desk Responses: A Comparative Study of Information-gathering Approaches* |
| | Yuval Marom and Ingrid Zukerman |
| 12:30-2:00 | Lunch |
| | **Session 4: Evaluation** |
| 2:00–2:25 | *DUC 2005: Evaluation of Question-Focused Summarization Systems* |
| | Hoa Trang Dang |
| 2:25–3:30 | Panel, Evaluation Programs: Hoa Trang Dang, Eduard Hovy, Noriko Kando |
| 3:30–4:00 | Break |
| | **Session 5: Multilingual Summarization Evaluation (MSE) 2006** |
| 4:00-4:30 | *Overview of MSE and Evaluation Results* by John Conroy |
| 4:30-5:10 | Invited Presentations from MSE participants |
| 5:10-5:30 | Discussion of Multilingual Summarization |

# Dimensionality Reduction Aids Term Co-Occurrence Based Multi-Document Summarization

**Ben Hachey, Gabriel Murray & David Reitter**
School of Informatics
University of Edinburgh
2 Buccleuch Place, Edinburgh EH8 9LW
bhachey@inf.ed.ac.uk, gabriel.murray@ed.ac.uk, dreitter@inf.ed.ac.uk

**Abstract**

A key task in an extraction system for query-oriented multi-document summarisation, necessary for computing relevance and redundancy, is modelling text semantics. In the Embra system, we use a representation derived from the singular value decomposition of a term co-occurrence matrix. We present methods to show the reliability of performance improvements. We find that Embra performs better with dimensionality reduction.

## 1 Introduction

We present experiments on the task of query-oriented multi-document summarisation as explored in the DUC 2005 and DUC 2006 shared tasks, which aim to model real-world complex question-answering. Input consists of a detailed query[1] and a set of 25 to 50 relevant documents. We implement an extractive approach where pieces of the original texts are selected to form a summary and then smoothing is performed to create a discursively coherent summary text.

The key modelling task in the extraction phase of such a system consists of estimating responsiveness to the query and avoiding redundancy. Both of these are often approached through some textual measure of semantic similarity. In the Embra[2] system, we follow this approach in a sentence extraction framework. However, we model the semantics of a sentence using a very large distributional semantics (i.e. term co-occurrence) space reduced by singular value decomposition. Our hypothesis is that this dimensionality reduction using a large corpus can outperform a simple term co-occurrence model.

A number of papers in the literature look at singular value decomposition and compare it to unreduced term × document or term co-occurrence matrix representations. These explore varied tasks and obtain mixed results. For example, Pedersen et al. (2005) find that SVD does not improve performance in a name discrimination task while Matveeva et al. (2005) and Rohde et al. (In prep) find that dimensionality reduction with SVD does help on word similarity tasks.

The experiments contained herein investigate the contribution of singular value decomposition on the query-oriented multi-document summarisation task. We compare the singular value decomposition of a term co-occurrence matrix derived from a corpus of approximately 100 million words (DS+SVD) to an unreduced version of the matrix (DS). These representations are described in Section 2. Next, Section 3 contains a discussion of related work using SVD for summarisation and a description of the sentence selection component in the Embra system. The paper goes on to give an overview of the experimental design and results in Section 4. This includes a detailed analysis of the statistical significance of the results.

## 2 Representing Sentence Semantics

The following three subsections discuss various ways of representing sentence meaning for information extraction purposes. While the first approach relies solely on weighted term frequencies in a vector space, the subsequent methods attempt to use term context information to better represent the meanings of sentences.

[1] On average, queries contain approximately 34 words words and three sentences.

[2] Edinburgh Multi-document Breviloquence Assay



*Proceedings of the Workshop on Task-Focused Summarization and Question Answering*, pages 1–7,
Sydney, July 2006. 

### 2.1 Terms and Term Weighting (TF.IDF)

The traditional model for measuring semantic similarity in information retrieval and text mining is based on a vector representation of the distribution of terms in documents. Within the vector space model, each term is assigned a weight which signifies the semantic importance of the term. Often, *tf.idf* is used for this weight, which is a scheme that combines the importance of a term within the current document[3] and the distribution of the term across the text collection. The former is often represented by the term frequency and the latter by the inverse document frequency ($idf_i = \frac{N}{df_i}$), where $N$ is the number of documents and $df_i$ is the number of documents containing term $t_i$.

### 2.2 Term Co-occurrence (DS)

Another approach eschews the traditional vector space model in favour of the distributional semantics approach. The DS model is based on the intuition that two words are semantically similar if they appear in a similar set of contexts. We can obtain a representation of a document's semantics by averaging the context vectors of the document terms. (See Besançon et al. (1999), where the DS model is contrasted with a term $\times$ document vector space representation.)

### 2.3 Singular Value Decomposition (DS+SVD)

Our third approach uses dimensionality reduction. Singular value decomposition is a technique for dimensionality reduction that has been used extensively for the analysis of lexical semantics under the name of latent semantic analysis (Landauer et al., 1998). Here, a rectangular (e.g., term $\times$ document) matrix is decomposed into the product of three matrices ($X_{w \times p} = W_{w \times n} S_{n \times n} (P_{p \times n})^T$) with $n$ 'latent semantic' dimensions. $W$ and $P$ represent terms and documents in the new space. And $S$ is a diagonal matrix of singular values in decreasing order.

Taking the product $W_{w \times k} S_{k \times k} (P_{p \times k})^T$ over the first $k$ columns gives the best least square approximation of the original matrix $X$ by a matrix of rank $k$, i.e. a reduction of the original matrix to $k$ dimensions. Similarity between documents can then be computed in the space obtained by taking the rank $k$ product of $S$ and $P$.

[3]The local importance of a term can also be computed over other textual units, e.g. sentence in extractive summarisation or the context of an entity pair in relation discovery.

This decomposition abstracts away from terms and can be used to model a semantic similarity that is more linguistic in nature. Furthermore, it has been successfully used to model human intuitions about meaning. For example, Landauer et al. (1998) show that latent semantic analysis correlates well with human judgements of word similarity and Foltz (1998) shows that it is a good estimator for textual coherence.

It is hoped that these latter two techniques (dimensionality reduction and the DS model) will provide for a more robust representation of term contexts and therefore better representation of sentence meaning, enabling us to achieve more reliable sentence similarity measurements for extractive summarisation.

## 3 SVD in Summarisation

This section describes ways in which SVD has been used for summarisation and details the implementation in the Embra system.

### 3.1 Related Work

In seminal work by Gong and Liu (2001), the authors proposed that the rows of $P^T$ may be regarded as defining topics, with the columns representing sentences from the document. In their SVD method, summarisation proceeds by choosing, for each row in $P^T$, the sentence with the highest value. This process continues until the desired summary length is reached.

Steinberger and Ježek (2004) have offered two criticisms of the Gong and Liu approach. Firstly, the method described above ties the dimensionality reduction to the desired summary length. Secondly, a sentence may score highly but never "win" in any dimension, and thus will not be extracted despite being a good candidate. Their solution is to assign each sentence an SVD-based score using:

$$Sc_i^{SVD} = \sqrt{\sum_{i=1}^{n} v(i,k)^2 * \sigma(k)^2},$$

where $v(i,k)$ is the $k$th element of the $i$th sentence vector and $\sigma(k)$ is the corresponding singular value.

Murray et al. (2005a) address the same concerns but retain the Gong and Liu framework. Rather than extracting the best sentence for each topic, the $n$ best sentences are extracted, with $n$ determined by the corresponding singular values from matrix $S$. Thus, dimensionality reduction is no longer tied to summary length and more than one sentence per topic can be chosen.

A similar approach in DUC 2005 using term co-occurrence models and SVD was presented by Jagarlamudi et al. (2005). Their system performs SVD over a term × sentence matrix and combines a relevance measurement based on this representation with relevance based on a term co-occurrence model by a weighted linear combination.

### 3.2 Sentence Selection in Embra

The Embra system developed for DUC 2005 attempts to derive more robust representations of sentences by building a large semantic space using SVD on a very large corpus. While researchers have used such large semantic spaces to aid in automatically judging the coherence of documents (Foltz et al., 1998; Barzilay and Lapata, 2005), to our knowledge this is a novel technique in summarisation.

Using a concatenation of Aquaint and DUC 2005 data (100+ million words), we utilised the Infomap tool[4] to build a semantic model based on singular value decomposition (SVD). The decomposition and projection of the matrix to a lower-dimensionality space results in a semantic model based on underlying term relations. In the current experiments, we set dimension of the reduced representation to 100. This is a reduction of 90% from the full dimensionality of 1000 content-bearing terms in the original DS matrix. This was found to perform better than 25, 50, 250 and 500 during parameter optimisation. A given sentence is represented as a vector which is the average of its constituent word vectors. This sentence representation is then fed into an MMR-style algorithm.

MMR (Maximal Marginal Relevance) is a common approach for determining relevance and redundancy in multi-document summarisation, in which candidate sentences are represented as weighted term-frequency vectors which can thus be compared to query vectors to gauge similarity and already-extracted sentence vectors to gauge redundancy, via the cosine of the vector pairs (Carbonell and Goldstein, 1998). While this has proved successful to a degree, the sentences are represented merely according to weighted term frequency in the document, and so two similar sentences stand a chance of not being considered similar if they do not share the same terms.

```
for each sentence in document:
    for each word in sentence:
        get word vector from semantic model
    average word vectors to form sentence vector
    sim1 = cossim(sentence vector, query vector)
    sim2 = highest(cossim(sentence vector, all extracted vectors))
    score = λ*sim1 - (1-λ)*sim2
extract sentence with highest score
repeat until desired length
```

Figure 1: Sentence extraction algorithm

Our implementation of MMR (Figure 1) uses $\lambda$ annealing following (Murray et al., 2005a). $\lambda$ decreases as the summary length increases, thereby emphasising relevance at the outset but increasingly prioritising redundancy removal as the process continues.

## 4 Experiment

The experimental setup uses the DUC 2005 data (Dang, 2005) and the Rouge evaluation metric to explore the hypothesis that query-oriented multi-document summarisation using a term co-occurrence representation can be improved using SVD. We frame the research question as follows:

> Does SVD dimensionality reduction lead to an increase in Rouge score compared to the DS representation?

### 4.1 Materials

The DUC 2005 task[5] was motivated by Amigo et al.'s (2004) suggestion of evaluations that model real-world complex question answering. The goal is to synthesise a well-organised, fluent answer of no more than 250 words to a complex question from a set of 25 to 50 relevant documents. The data includes a detailed query, a document set, and at least 4 human summaries for each of 50 topics.

The preprocessing was largely based on LT TTT and LT XML tools (Grover et al., 2000; Thompson et al., 1997). First, we perform tokenisation and sentence identification. This is followed by lemmatisation.

At the core of preprocessing is the LT TTT program *fsgmatch*, a general purpose transducer which processes an input stream and adds annotations using rules provided in a hand-written grammar file. We also use the statistical combined part-of-speech (POS) tagger and sentence boundary disambiguation module from LT TTT (Mikheev,

[4] `http://infomap.stanford.edu/`

[5] `http://www-nlpir.nist.gov/projects/duc/duc2005/tasks.html`

1997). Using these tools, we produce an XML markup with sentence and word elements. Further linguistic markup is added using the *morpha* lemmatiser (Minnen et al., 2000) and the *C&C* named entity tagger (Curran and Clark, 2003) trained on the data from MUC-7.

### 4.2 Methods

The different system configurations (DS, DS+SVD, TF.IDF) were evaluated against the human upper bound and a baseline using Rouge-2 and Rouge-SU4. Rouge estimates the coverage of appropriate concepts (Lin and Hovy, 2003) in a summary by comparing it several human-created reference summaries. Rouge-2 does so by computing precision and recall based on macro-averaged bigram overlap. Rouge-SU4 allows bigrams to be composed of non-contiguous words, with as many as four words intervening. We use the same configuration as the official DUC 2005 evaluation,[6] which is based on word stems (rather than full forms) and uses jackknifing ($k-1$ cross-evaluation) so that human gold-standard and automatic system summaries can be compared.

The independent variable in the experiment is the model of sentence semantics used by the sentence selection algorithm. We are primarily interested in the relative performance of the DS and DS+SVD representations. As well as this, we include the DUC 2005 baseline, which is a lead summary created by taking the first 250 words of the most recent document for each topic. We also include a *tf.idf*-weighted term × sentence representation (TF.IDF) for comparison with a conventional MMR approach.[7] Finally, we include an upper bound calculated using the DUC 2005 human reference summaries. Preprocessing and all other aspects of the sentence selection algorithm remain constant over all systems.

In general, Rouge shows a large variance across data sets (and so does system performance). It is important to test whether obtained nominal differences are due to chance or are actually statistically significant.

To test whether the Rouge metric showed a reliably different performance for the systems, the Friedman rank sum test (Friedman, 1940; Demšar, 2006) can be used. This is a hypothesis test not unlike an ANOVA, however, it is non-parametric, i.e. it does not assume a normal distribution of the measures (i.e. precision, recall and F-score). More importantly, it does not require homogeneity of variances.

To (partially) rank the systems against each other, we used a cascade of Wilcoxon signed ranks tests. These tests are again non-parametric (as they rank the differences between the system results for the datasets). As discussed by Demšar (2006), we used Holm's procedure for multiple tests to correct our error estimates ($p$).

| p | Metric | hypothesis |
|---|---|---|
| 0.000262 | Rouge-2 | base<TF.IDF *** |
| 0.021640 | Rouge-2 | base<DS * |
| 0.000508 | Rouge-2 | base<DS+SVD *** |
| 0.014845 | Rouge-2 | DS<TF.IDF * |
| 0.507702 | Rouge-2 | TF.IDF<DS+SVD |
| 0.047016 | Rouge-2 | DS<DS+SVD * |
| 0.000080 | Rouge-SU4 | base<TF.IDF *** |
| 0.006803 | Rouge-SU4 | base<DS ** |
| 0.000006 | Rouge-SU4 | base<DS+SVD *** |
| 0.012815 | Rouge-SU4 | DS<TF.IDF * |
| 0.320083 | Rouge-SU4 | TF.IDF<DS+SVD |
| 0.001053 | Rouge-SU4 | DS<DS+SVD ** |

Table 1: Holm-corrected Wilcoxon hypothesis test results.

### 4.3 Results

Friedman tests for each Rouge metric (with F-score, precision and recall included as observations, with the dataset as group) showed a reliable effect of the system configuration ($\chi^2_{F,SU4} = 106.6$, $\chi^2_{P,SU4} = 96.1$, $\chi^2_{R,SU4} = 105.5$, all $p < 0.00001$).

Post-hoc analysis (Wilcoxon) showed (see Table 1) that all three systems performed reliably better than the baseline. TF.IDF performed better than simple DS in Rouge-2 and Rouge-SU4. DS+SVD performed better than DS ($p_2 < 0.05$, $p_{SU4} < 0.005$). There is no evidence to support a claim that DS+SVD performed differently from TF.IDF.

However, when we specifically compared the performance of TF.IDF and DS+SVD with the Rouge-SU4 F score for only the specific (as opposed to general) summaries, we found that DS+SVD scored reliably, but only slightly better

[6] i.e. `ROUGE-1.5.5.pl -n 2 -x -m -2 4 -u -c 95 -r 1000 -f A -p 0.5 -t 0 d`

[7] Specifically, we use $tf_{i,j} * log(\frac{N}{df_i})$ for term weighting where $tf_{i,j}$ is the number of times term $i$ occurs in sentence $j$, $N$ is the number of sentences, and $df_i$ is the number of sentences containing term $i$.

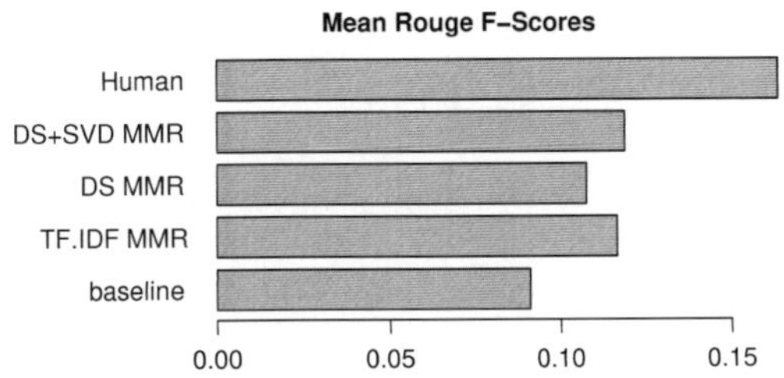


Figure 2: Mean system performance over 50 datasets (F-scores). Precision and Recall look qualitatively similar.

(Wilcoxon, $p<0.05$). This result is unadjusted, and post-hoc comparisons with other scores or for the general summaries did not show reliable differences.

Having established the reliable performance improvement of DS+SVD over DS, it it important to take the effect size into consideration (with enough data, small effects may be statistically significant, but practically unimportant). Figure 2 illustrates that the gain in mean performance is substantial. If the mean Rouge-SU4 score for human performance is seen as upper bound, the DS+SVD system showed a 25.4 percent reduction in error compared to the DS system.[8]

A similar analysis for precision and recall gives qualitatively comparable results.

## 5 Discussion and Future Work

The positive message from the experimental results is that SVD dimensionality reduction improves performance over a term co-occurrence model for computing relevance and redundancy in a MMR framework. We note that we cannot conclude that the DS or DS+SVD systems outperform a conventional *tf.idf*-weighted term × sentence representation on this task. However, results from Jagarlamudi et al. (2005) suggest that the DS and term × sentence representations may be complementary in which case we would expect a further improvement through an ensemble technique.

Previous results comparing SVD with unreduced representations show mixed results. For example, Pedersen et al. (2005) experiment with term co-occurrence representations with and without SVD on a name discrimination task and find that the unreduced representation tends to perform better. Rohde et al. (In prep), on the other hand, find that a reduced matrix does perform better on word pair similarity and multiple-choice vocabulary tests. One crucial factor here may be the size of the corpus. SVD may not offer any reliable 'latent semantic' advantage when the corpus is small, in which case the efficiency gain from dimensionality reduction is less of a motivation anyway.

We plan to address the question of corpus size in future work by comparing DS and DS+SVD derived from corpora of varying size. We hypothesise that the larger the corpus used to compile the term co-occurrence information, the larger the potential contribution from dimensionality reduction. This will be explored by running the experiment described in this paper a number of times using corpora of different sizes (e.g. 0.5m, 1m, 10m and 100m words).

Unlike official DUC evaluations, which rely on human judgements of readability and informativeness, our experiments rely solely on Rouge $n$-gram evaluation metrics. It has been shown in DUC 2005 and in work by Murray et al. (2005b; 2006) that Rouge does not always correlate well with human evaluations, though there is more stability when examining the correlations of macro-averaged scores. Rouge suffers from a lack of power to discriminate between systems whose performance is judged to differ by human annotators. Thus, it is likely that future human evaluations would be more informative. Another way that the evaluation issue might be addressed is by using an annotated sentence extraction corpus. This could proceed by comparing gold standard alignments between abstract and full document sentences with predicted alignments using correlation analysis.

## 6 Conclusions

We have presented experiments with query-oriented multi-document summarisation. The experiments explore the question of whether SVD dimensionality reduction offers any improvement over a term co-occurrence representation for sentence semantics for measuring relevance and redundancy. While the experiments show that our system does not outperform a term × sentence *tf.idf* system, we have shown that the SVD reduced representation of a term co-occurrence space built from a large corpora performs better than the unreduced representation. This contra-

[8]Pairwise effect size estimates over datasets aren't sensible. Averaging of differences between pairs was affected by outliers, presumably caused by Rouge's error distribution.

dicts related work where SVD did not provide an improvement over unreduced representations on the name discrimination task (Pedersen et al., 2005). However, it is compatible with other work where SVD has been shown to help on the task of estimating human notions of word similarity (Matveeva et al., 2005; Rohde et al., In prep). A detailed analysis using the Friedman test and a cascade of Wilcoxon signed ranks tests suggest that our results are statistically valid despite the unreliability of the Rouge evaluation metric due to its low variance across systems.

## Acknowledgements

This work was supported in part by Scottish Enterprise Edinburgh-Stanford Link grant R36410 and, as part of the EASIE project, grant R37588. It was also supported in part by the European Union 6th FWP IST Integrated Project AMI (Augmented Multiparty Interaction, FP6-506811, publication).

We would like to thank James Clarke for detailed comments and discussion. We would also like to thank the anonymous reviewers for their comments.

## References

Enrique Amigo, Julio Gonzalo, Victor Peinado, Anselmo Penas, and Felisa Verdejo. 2004. An empirical study of information synthesis tasks. In *Proceedings of the 42nd Annual Meeting of the Association for Computational Linguistics*, Barcelona, Spain.

Regina Barzilay and Mirella Lapata. 2005. Modeling local coherence: an entity-based approach. In *Proceedings of the 43rd Annual Meeting of the Association for Computational Linguistics*, Ann Arbor, MI, USA.

Romaric Besançon, Martin Rajman, and Jean-Cédric Chappelier. 1999. Textual similarities based on a distributional approach. In *Proceedings of the 10th International Workshop on Database And Expert Systems Applications*, Firenze, Italy.

Jaime G. Carbonell and Jade Goldstein. 1998. The use of mmr, diversity-based reranking for reordering documents and producing summaries. In *Proceedings of the 21st Annual International ACM SIGIR Conference on Research and Development in Information Retrieval*, Melbourne, Australia.

James R. Curran and Stephen Clark. 2003. Language independent NER using a maximum entropy tagger. In *Proceedings of the 2003 Conference on Computational Natural Language Learning*, Edmonton, Canada.

Hoa T. Dang. 2005. Overview of DUC 2005. In *Proceedings of the Document Understanding Conference*, Vancouver, B.C., Canada.

Janez Demšar. 2006. Statistical comparisons of classifiers over multiple data sets. *Journal of Machine Learning Research*, 7:1–30, Jan.

Peter W. Foltz, Walter Kintsch, and Thomas K. Landauer. 1998. The measurement of textual coherence with latent semantic analysis. *Discourse Processes*, 25.

Milton Friedman. 1940. A comparison of alternative tests of significance for the problem of m rankings. *The Annals of Mathematical Statistics*, 11:86–92.

Yihon Gong and Xin Liu. 2001. Generic text summarization using relevance measure and latent semantic analysis. In *Proceedings of the 24th Annual International ACM SIGIR Conference on Research and Development in Information Retrieval*, New Orleans, LA, USA.

Claire Grover, Colin Matheson, Andrei Mikheev, and Marc Moens. 2000. LT TTT—a flexible tokenisation tool. In *Proceedings of the 2nd International Conference on Language Resources and Evaluation*, Athens, Greece.

Ben Hachey and Claire Grover. 2004. A rhetorical status classifier for legal text summarisation. In *Proceedings of the ACL-2004 Text Summarization Branches Out Workshop*, Barcelona, Spain.

Jagadeesh Jagarlamudi, Prasad Pingali, and Vasudeva Varma. 2005. A relevance-based language modeling approach to DUC 2005. In *Proceedings of the Document Understanding Conference*, Vancouver, B.C., Canada.

Thomas K. Landauer, Peter W. Foltz, and Darrell Laham. 1998. Introduction to latent semantic analysis. *Discourse Processes*, 25.

Chin-Yew Lin and Eduard H. Hovy. 2003. Automatic evaluation of summaries using n-gram co-occurrence statistics. In *Proceedings of the Joint Human Language Technology Conference and North American Chapter of the Association for Computational Linguistics Annual Meeting*, Edmonton, Alberta, Canada.

Irina Matveeva, Gina-Anne Levow, Ayman Farahat, and Christiaan Royer. 2005. Term represetation with generalized latent semantic analysis. In *Proceedings of the 2005 Conference on Recent Advances in Natural Language Processing*, Borovets, Bulgaria.

Andrei Mikheev. 1997. Automatic rule induction for unknown word guessing. *Computational Linguistics*, 23(3).

Guido Minnen, John Carroll, and Darren Pearce. 2000. Robust, applied morphological generation. In *Proceedings of the 1st International Natural Language Generation Conference*, Mitzpe Ramon, Israel.

Gabriel Murray, Steve Renals, and Jean Carletta. 2005a. Extractive summarization of meeting recordings. In *Proceedings of the 9th European Conference on Speech Communication and Technology*, Lisbon, Portugal.

Gabriel Murray, Steve Renals, Jean Carletta, and Johanna Moore. 2005b. Evaluating automatic summaries of meeting recordings. In *Proceedings of the 43rd Annual Meeting of the Association for Computational Linguistics*, Ann Arbor, MI, USA.

Gabriel Murray, Steve Renals, Jean Carletta, and Johanna Moore. 2006. Incorporating speaker and discourse features into speech summarization. In *Proceedings of the Joint Human Language Technology Conference and North American Chapter of the Association for Computational Linguistics Annual Meeting*, New York City, NY, USA.

Ted Pedersen, Amruta Purandare, and Anagha Kulkarni. 2005. Name discrimination by clustering similar contexts. In *Proceedings of the 6th International Conference on Intelligent Text Processing and Computational Linguistics*, Mexico City, Mexico.

Douglas L. T. Rohde, Laur M. Gonnerman, and David C. Plaut. In prep. An improved method for deriving word meaning from lexical co-occurrence. `http://dlt4.mit.edu/~dr/COALS/Coals.pdf` (1 May 2006).

Josef Steinberger and Karel Ježek. 2004. Using latent semantic analysis in text summarization and summary evaluation. In *Proceedings of the 5th International Conference on Information Systems Implementation and Modelling*, Ostrava, Czech Republic.

Henry Thompson, Richard Tobin, David McKelvie, and Chris Brew. 1997. LT XML: Software API and toolkit for XML processing. *http://www.ltg.ed.ac.uk/software/*.

# Challenges in Evaluating Summaries of Short Stories

**Anna Kazantseva**
School of Information Technology
and Engineering,
University of Ottawa, Ottawa, Canada
ankazant@site.uottawa.ca

**Stan Szpakowicz**
School of Information Technology
and Engineering,
University of Ottawa, Ottawa, Canada
Institute of Computer Science,
Polish Academy of Sciences, Warsaw, Poland
szpak@site.uottawa.ca

## Abstract

This paper presents experiments with the evaluation of automatically produced summaries of literary short stories. The summaries are tailored to a particular purpose of helping a reader decide whether she wants to read the story. The evaluation procedure includes extrinsic and intrinsic measures, as well as subjective and factual judgments about the summaries pronounced by human subjects. The experiments confirm the experience of summarizing more conventional genres: sentence overlap between human- and machine-made summaries is not a complete picture of the quality of a summary. In fact, in our case, sentence overlap does not correlate well with human judgment. We explain the evaluation procedures and discuss several challenges of evaluating summaries of works of fiction.

## 1 Introduction

In recent years the automatic text summarization community has increased its focus on reliable evaluation. The much used evaluation methods based on sentence overlap with reference summaries have been called into question (Mani 2001) as they provide only a rough approximation of semantic similarity between summaries. A number of deeper, more semantically-motivated approaches have been proposed, such as the factoid method (van Halteren and Teufel, 2003) and the pyramid method (Nenkova and Passonneau 2004). These methods measure similarity between reference and generated summaries more reliably but, unfortunately, have a disadvantage of being very labour-intensive.

This paper describes experiments in evaluating automatically produced summaries of literary short stories. It presents an approach that evaluates summaries from two different perspectives: comparing computer-made summaries to those produced by humans based on sentence-overlap and measuring usefulness and informativeness of the summaries by themselves – a step critical when creating and evaluating summaries of a relatively unexplored genre. The paper also points out several challenges specific to evaluating summaries of fiction such as questionable suitability of traditional metrics (those based on sentence overlap), unavailability of clearly defined criteria to judge "goodness" of a summary and a higher degree of redundancy in such texts.

We achieve these goals by performing a two-step evaluation of our summaries. Initially, for each story in the test set we compare sentence overlap between summaries which the system generates and those produced by three human subjects. These experiments reveal that inter-rater agreement measures tend to be pessimistic where fiction is concerned. This seems due to a higher degree of redundancy and paraphrasing in such texts. The second stage of the evaluation process seeks to measure usefulness of the summaries in a more tangible way. To this end, three subjects answered a number of questions, first after



*Proceedings of the Workshop on Task-Focused Summarization and Question Answering*, pages 8–15,
Sydney, July 2006. 

**Figure 1. Example of a summary produced by the system.**
A MATTER OF MEAN ELEVATION. By O. Henry (1862-1910).
On the camino real along the beach the two saddle mules and the four pack mules of Don Señor Johnny Armstrong stood, patiently awaiting the crack of the whip of the arriero, Luis. These articles Don Johnny traded to the interior Indians for the gold dust that they washed from the Andean streams and stored in quills and bags against his coming. It was a profitable business, and Señor Armstrong expected soon to be able to purchase the coffee plantation that he coveted. Armstrong stood on the narrow sidewalk, exchanging garbled Spanish with old Peralto, the rich native merchant who had just charged him four prices for half a gross of pot-metal hatchets, and abridged English with Rucker, the little German who was Consul for the United States. [...] Armstrong, waved a good-bye and took his place at the tail of the procession. Armstrong concurred, and they turned again upward toward Tacuzama. [...] Peering cautiously inside, he saw, within three feet of him, a woman of marvellous, imposing beauty, clothed in a splendid loose robe of leopard skins. The hut was packed close to the small space in which she stood with the squatting figures of Indians. [...] I am an American. If you need assistance tell me how I can render it. [...] The woman was worthy of his boldness. Only by a sudden flush of her pale cheek did she acknowledge understanding of his words. [...] " I am held a prisoner by these Indians. God knows I need help. [...] look, Mr. Armstrong, there is the sea!

reading only the summary and then after reading the complete story. The set included both factual questions (e.g. *can you tell where this story takes place?*) and subjective questions (e.g. *how readable did you find this summary?*).

Finally, we compare the two types of results with a surprising discovery: overlap-based measures and human judgment do not correlate well in our case.

This paper is organized in the following manner. **Section 2** briefly describes our summarizer of short stories. **Section 3.1** discusses experiments comparing generated summaries to reference ones based on sentence overlap. The experiments involving human judgment of the summaries are presented in **Section 3.2** and the two types of experiments are compared in **Section 3.3**. **Section 4** draws conclusions and outlines possible directions for future work.

## 2 Background: System Description

A detailed description of our summarizer of short stories is outside the scope of this paper. For completeness, this section gives an overview of the system's inner workings. An interested reader is referred to our previous work (Kazantseva 2006) for more information.

The system is designed to create a particular type of indicative generic summaries – namely, summaries that would help readers decide whether they would like to read a given story. Because of this, a summary, as defined here, is not meant to summarize the plot of a story. It is intended to raise adequate expectations and to enable a reader to make informed decisions based on a summary only. We achieve this goal by identifying the salient portions of the original texts that lay out the setting of a story, namely, location and main characters. The present prototype of our system creates summaries by extracting sentences from original documents. An example summary produced by the system appears in **Figure 1**.

The system works in two stages. First it attempts to identify important entities in stories (locations and characters). Next, sentences that are descriptive and set out the background of a story are separated from those that relate events of the plot. Finally, the system selects summary-worthy sentences in a way that favours descriptive ones that focus on important entities and occur early in the text.

The identification of important entities is achieved by processing the stories using a gazetteer. Pronominal and noun phrase anaphora are very common in fiction, so we resolve anaphoric expressions of these two types. The anaphora resolution module is restricted to resolving singular anaphoric expressions that denote animate entities (people and, sometimes, animals). The main characters are then identified using normalized frequency counts.

The next stage of the process attempts to identify sentences that set out the background in each story. The stories are parsed using the Connexor Machinese Syntax Parser (Tapanainen and Järvinen 1997) and sentences are split into clauses.

Each clause is represented as a vector of features that approximate its aspectual type. The features are designed to help identify state clauses (*John was a tall man*) and serial situations (*John always drops things*) (Huddleston and Pullum 2002, p. 123-124).

Four groups of features represent each clause: character-related, location-related, aspect-related and others. Character-related features capture such information as the presence of a mention of one of the main characters in a clause, its syntactic function, how early in the text this mention occurs, etc. Location-related features state whether a clause contains a location name and whether this name is embedded in a prepositional phrase. Aspect-related features reflect a number of properties of a clause that influence its aspectual type. They include the main verb's lexical aspect, the tense, the presence and the type of temporal expressions, voice, and the presence of modal verbs.

In our experiments we create two separate representations for each clause: fine-grained and coarse-grained. Both contain features from all four feature groups. The difference between them is only in the number of features and in the cardinality of the set of possible values.

Two different procedures achieve the actual selection process. The first procedure performs decision tree induction using C5.0 (Quinlan 1992) to select the most likely candidate sentences. The training data for this process consists of short stories annotated at the clause-level by the first author of this paper. The second procedure applies a set of manually created rules to select summary-worthy sentences.

The corpus for the experiments contains 47 short stories from Project Gutenberg (http://www.gutenberg.org) divided into a training set (27 stories) and a test set (20 stories). These are classical works written in English or translated into English by authors including O.Henry, Jerome K. Jerome, Katherine Mansfield and Anton Chekhov. They have on average 3,333 tokens and 244 sentences (4.5 letter-sized pages). The target compression rate was set at 6% counted in sentences. This rate was selected because it corresponded to the compression rate achieved by the first author when creating initial training and test data.

## 3 Evaluation: Experimental Setup

We designed our evaluation procedure to have easily interpreted, meaningful results, and keep the amount of labour reasonable. We worked with six subjects (different than the authors of this paper) who performed two separate tasks.

In Task 1 each subject was asked to read a story and create its summary by selecting 6% of the sentences. The subjects were explained that their summaries were to raise expectations about the story, but not to reveal what happens in it.

In Task 2 the subjects made a number of judgments about the summaries before and after reading the original stories. The subjects read a summary similar to the one shown in **Figure 1**. Next, they were asked six questions, three of which were factual in nature and three others were subjective. The subjects had to answer these questions using the summary as the only source of information. Subsequently, they read the original story and answered almost the same questions (see **Section 4**). This process allowed us to understand how informative the summaries were by themselves, without access to the originals, and also whether they were misleading or incomplete.

The experiments were performed on a test set of 20 stories and involved six participants divided into two groups of three people. Group 1 performed Task 1 on stories 1-10 of the testing set and Group 2 performed this task on stories 11-20. During Task 2 Group 1 worked on stories 11-20 and Group 2 – on stories 1-10.

By adjusting a number of system parameters, we produced four different summaries per story. All four versions were compared with human-made summaries using sentence overlap-based measures. However, because the experiments are rather time consuming, it was not possible to evaluate more than one set of summaries using human judgments (Task 2). That is why only summaries generated using the coarse-grained dataset and manually composed rules were evaluated in Task 2. We selected this version because the differences between this set of summaries and gold-standard summaries are easiest to interpret. That is to say, decisions based on a set of rules employing a smaller number of parameters are easier to track than those taken using machine learning or more elaborate rules.

On average, the subjects reported that completing both tasks required between 15 and 35 hours of work. Four out of six subjects were native speakers of English. Two others had a near-native and very good levels of English respectively. The participants were given the data in form of files and had four weeks to complete the tasks.

### 3.1 Creating Gold-Standard Summaries: Task 1

During this task each participant had to create extract-based summaries for 10 different stories. The criteria (making a summary indicative rather than informative) were explained and one example of an annotated story shown. The instructions for these experiments are available at <http://www.site.uottawa.ca/~ankazant/instructions.zip>.

**Table 1** presents several measures of agreement between judges within each group and with the first author of this paper (included in the agreement figures because this person created the initial training data and test data for the preliminary experiments).

The measurement names are displayed in the first column of **Table 1**. *Cohen* denotes Cohen's kappa (Cohen 1960). *PABAK* denotes Prevalence and Bias Adjusted Kappa (Bland and Altman 1986). *ICC* denotes Intra-class Correlation Coefficient (Shrout and Fleiss 1979). The numbers *3* and *4* state whether the statistic is computed only for 3 subjects participating in the evaluation or for 4 subjects (including the first author of the paper).

**Table 1. Inter-judge agreement.**

| Statistic | Group 1 | Group 2 | Average |
|---|---|---|---|
| Cohen (4) | 0.50 | 0.34 | 0.42 |
| Cohen (3) | 0.51 | 0.34 | 0.42 |
| PABAK (4) | 0.88 | 0.85 | 0.87 |
| PABAK (3) | 0.89 | 0.86 | 0.87 |
| ICC (4) | 0.80 (0.78, 0.82) | 0.67 (0.64, 0.70) | 0.73 (0.71, 0.76) |
| ICC (3) | 0.76 (0.74, 0.80) | 0.6 (0.56, 0.64) | 0.68 (0.65, 0.72) |

As can be seen in **Table 1**, the agreement statistics are computed for each group separately. This is because the sets of stories that they annotated are disjoint. The column *Average* provides an average of these figures to give a better overall idea.

Cohen's kappa in its original form can only be computed for a pair of raters. For this reason we computed it for each possible pair-wise combination of raters within a group and then the numbers were averaged. The PABAK statistic was computed in the same manner using Cohen's kappa as its basis. ICC is the statistic that measures inter-rater agreement and can be computed for more than 2 judges. It was computed for all 3 or 4 raters at the same time. ICC was computed for a two-way mixed model and measures the average reliability of ratings taken together. The numbers in parentheses are confidence intervals for 99% confidence.

We compute three different agreement measures because each of these statistics has its weakness and distorts the results in a different manner. Cohen's kappa is known to be a pessimistic measurement in the presence of a severe class imbalance, as is the case in our setting (Sim and Wright 2005). PABAK is a measure that takes class imbalance into account, but it is too optimistic because it artificially removes class imbalance present in the original setting. ICC has weaknesses similar to Cohen's kappa (sensitivity to class imbalance). Besides, it assumes that the sample of targets to be rated (sentences in our case) is a random sample of targets drawn from a larger population. This is not

**Figure 2. Fragments of summaries produced by 3 annotators for *The Cost of Kindness* by Jerome K Jerome.**

**Annotator A.**

The Rev. Augustus Cracklethorpe would be quitting Wychwood-on-the-Heaththe the following Monday, never to set foot [...] in the neighbourhood again. The Rev. Augustus Cracklethorpe, M.A., might possibly have been of service to his Church in, say, [...] some mission station far advanced amid the hordes of heathendom. In picturesque little Wychwood-on-the-Heath [...] these qualities made only for scandal and disunion. Churchgoers who had not visited St. Jude's for months had promised themselves the luxury of feeling they were listening to the Rev. Augustus Cracklethorpe for the last time. The Rev. Augustus Cracklethorpe had prepared a sermon that for plain speaking and directness was likely to leave an impression.

**Annotator B.**

The Rev. Augustus Cracklethorpe would be quitting Wychwood-on-the-Heaththe the following Monday, never to set foot [...] in the neighbourhood again. The Rev. Augustus Cracklethorpe, M.A., might possibly have been of service to his Church in, say, [..] some mission station far advanced amid the hordes of heathendom. What marred the entire business was the impulsiveness of little Mrs. Pennycoop. Mr. Pennycoop, carried away by his wife's eloquence, added a few halting words of his own. Other ladies felt it their duty to show to Mrs. Pennycoop that she was not the only Christian in Wychwood-on-the-Heath.

**Annotator C.**

The Rev. Augustus Cracklethorpe would be quitting Wychwood-on-the-Heath the following Monday, never to set foot [...] in the neighbourhood again. The Rev. Augustus Cracklethorpe, M.A., might possibly have been of service to his Church in, say, [...] some mission station far advanced amid the hordes of heathendom. For the past two years the Rev. Cracklethorpe's parishioners [...] had sought to impress upon him, [..] their cordial and daily-increasing dislike of him, both as a parson and a man. The Rev. Augustus Cracklethorpe had prepared a sermon that for plain speaking and directness was likely to leave an impression. The parishioners of St. Jude's, Wychwood-on-the-Heath, had their failings, as we all have. The Rev. Augustus flattered himself that he had not missed out a single one, and was looking forward with pleasurable anticipation to the sensation that his remarks, from his "firstly" to his "sixthly and lastly," were likely to create.

necessarily the case as the corpus was not compiled randomly.

We hope that these three measures, although insufficient individually, provide an adequate understanding of inter-rater agreement in our evaluation. We note that the average overlap (intersection) between judges in each group is 1.8% out of 6% of summary-worthy sentences.

All of these agreement measures and, in fact, all measures based on computing sentence overlap are inherently incomplete where fiction is concerned because any two different sentences are not necessarily "equally different". The matter is exemplified in **Figure 2**. It displays segments of summaries produced for the same story by three different annotators. Computing Cohen's kappa between these fragments gives agreement of 0.521 between annotators A and B and 0.470 between annotators A and C. However, a closer look at these fragments reveals that there are more differences between summaries A and B than between summaries A and C. This is because many of the sentences in summaries A and C describe the same information (personal qualities of Rev. Cracklethorpe) even though they do not overlap. On the other hand, sentences from summaries A and B are not only distinct; they "talk" about different facts. This problem is not unique to fiction, but in this context it is more acute because literary texts exhibit more redundancy.

**Table 2. Sentence overlap between computer- and human-made summaries. Majority gold-standard.**

| Dataset | Prec. | Rec. | F |
|---|---|---|---|
| LEAD | 25.09 | 30.49 | 27.53 |
| LEAD CHAR | 28.14 | 33.18 | 30.45 |
| Rules, coarse-grained | 34.14 | 44.39 | 38.60 |
| Rules, fine-gr. | 39.27 | 50.00 | 43.99 |
| Machine learning, coarse-gr. | 35.55 | 40.81 | 38.00 |
| ML, fine-gr. | 37.97 | 50.22 | 43.22 |

**Tables 2-4** show the results of comparing four different versions of computer-made summaries against gold-standard summaries produced by humans. The tables also display the results of two baseline algorithms. The LEAD baseline refers to the version of summaries produced by selecting the first 6% of sentences in each story. LEAD CHAR baseline is obtained by selecting first

**Table 3. Sentence overlap between computer- and human-made summaries. Union gold-standard.**

| Dataset | Prec. | Rec. | F |
|---|---|---|---|
| LEAD | 36.53 | 17.97 | 24.09 |
| LEAD CHAR | 44.49 | 21.23 | 28.75 |
| Rules, coarse-grained | 52.41 | 30.96 | 38.92 |
| Rules, fine-gr. | 56.77 | 31.22 | 40.28 |
| Machine learning, coarse-gr. | 51.17 | 23.76 | 32.47 |
| ML, fine-gr. | 55.59 | 29.76 | 38.77 |

**Table 4. Sentence overlap between computer- and human-made summaries. Intersection gold-standard.**

| Dataset | Prec. | Rec. | F |
|---|---|---|---|
| LEAD | 12.55 | 37.36 | 18.78 |
| LEAD CHAR | 15.97 | 46.14 | 23.73 |
| Rules, coarse-grained | 19.66 | 62.64 | 29.92 |
| Rules, fine-gr. | 23.10 | 76.92 | 35.53 |
| Machine learning, coarse-gr. | 19.14 | 53.85 | 28.24 |
| ML, fine-gr. | 21.36 | 69.23 | 32.64 |

6% of sentences that contain a mention of an important character. The improvements over the baselines are significant with 99% confidence in all cases.

By combining summaries created by human annotators in different ways we create three distinct gold-standard summaries.

*The majority* gold-standard summary contains all sentences that were selected by at least two judges. It is the most commonly accepted way of creating gold-standard summaries and it is best suited to give an overall picture of how similar computer-made summaries are to man-made ones.

*The union* gold standard is obtained by considering all sentences that were judged summary-worthy by at least one judge. Union summaries provide a more relaxed measurement. Precision for the union gold standard gives one an idea of how many irrelevant sentences a given summary contains (sentences not selected by any of three judges are more likely to prove irrelevant).

The *intersection* summaries are obtained by combining sentences that all three judges deemed to be important. Intersection gold standard is the strictest way to measure the goodness of a summary. Recall for intersection gold standard tells one how many of the most important sentences were included in summaries by the system (sentences selected by all three judges are likely to be the most important ones).

It should be noted, however, that the numbers in **Tables 2-4** do not give a complete picture of the quality of the summaries for the same reason that the agreement measures do not reveal fully the extent of inter-judge agreement: sentences that are not part of the reference summaries are not necessarily equally unsuitable for inclusion in the summary.

### 3.2 Human Judgment of Computer-Made Summaries: Task 2

In order to evaluate one summary in Task 2, a participant had to read it and to answer six questions using the summary as the only source of information. The participant was then required to read the original story and to answer another six questions. The questions asked before and after reading the original were the same with one exception: question Q4 was replaced by Q11 (see **Table 6**.) The subjects were asked not to correct the answers after the fact.

**Table 5. Answers to factual questions.**

| Id | Question | After summary only | | After reading the original | |
|---|---|---|---|---|---|
| | | Mean | Std. dev | Mean | Std. dev. |
| Q1, Q7 | Please list up to 3 main characters in this story, in the order of importance (scale: -1 to 3) | 2.28 | 0.64 | 2.78 | 0.45 |
| Q2, Q8 | State where this story takes place. Be as specific as possible (scale: -1 to 3) | 1.78 | 1.35 | 2.60 | 0.91 |
| Q3, Q9 | Select a time period when this story takes place.(scale: 0 or 1) | 0.53 | 0.50 | 0.70 | 0.46 |

**Table 6. Answers to subjective questions.**

| Id | Question (scale: 1 to 6) | After summary only | | After reading the original | |
|---|---|---|---|---|---|
| | | Mean | Std. dev | Mean | Std. dev. |
| Q4 | How readable do you find this summary? | 4.43 | 1.39 | N/A | N/A |
| Q5, Q10 | How much irrelevant information does this summary contain? | 4.27 | 1.41 | 4.51 | 1.16 |
| Q11 | How complete is the summary? | N/A | N/A | 4.53 | 1.25 |
| Q6, Q12 | How helpful was this summary for deciding whether you would like to read the story or not? | 4.52 | 1.37 | 4.6 | 1.21 |

Three of the questions were factual and three others – subjective. **Table 5** displays the factual questions along with the resulting answers. The participants had to answer questions Q1 and Q2 in their own words and question Q3 was a multiple-choice question where a participant selected the century when the story took place. Q1 and Q2 were ranked on a scale from -1 to 3. A score of 3 means that the answer was complete and correct, 2 – slightly incomplete, 1 – very incomplete, 0 – a subject could not find the answer in the text and -1 if the person answered incorrectly. Q3 was ranked on a binary scale (0 or 1).

Questions Q3-Q7 asked the participants to pronounce a subjective judgment on a summary. These were multiple-choice questions where a participant needed to select a score from 1 to 6, with 1 indicating a strong negative property and 6 indicating a strong positive property. The questions and results appear in **Table 6**.

The results displayed in **Tables 5** and **6** suggest that the subjects can answer simple questions based on the summaries alone. They also seem to indicate that the subjects found the summaries quite helpful. It is interesting to note that even after reading complete stories the subjects are not always capable of answering the factual questions with perfect precision.

### 3.3 Putting Sentence Overlap and Human Judgment Together

In order to check whether the two types of statistics measure the same or different qualities of the summaries, we explored whether the two are correlated.

**Table 7** displays the values of Spearman rank correlation coefficient between median values of answers for questions from Task 2 and measurements obtained by comparing computer-made summaries against the majority gold-standard summaries. All questions, except Q10 (relevance) and Q11 (completeness) are those asked and answered using the summary as the only source of information. Sentence overlap values (F-score, precision and recall) were discretized (banded) in order to be used in this test. These results are based on the values obtained for 20 stories in the test set – a relatively small sample – which prohibits drawing definite conclusions. However, in most cases the correlation coefficient between human opinions and sentence overlap measurements is below the cut-off

**Table 7. Spearman rank correlation coefficient between sentence overlap measures and human judgments.**

| Question | Prec. | Rec. | F |
|---|---|---|---|
| Q1(main characters) | 0.09 | 0.29 | 0.17 |
| Q2(location) | 0.21 | 0.18 | 0.22 |
| Q3(time) | 0.38 | 0.28 | 0.34 |
| Q4(readability) | 0.47 | 0.31 | 0.50 |
| Q5(relevance) | 0.31 | 0.19 | 0.34 |
| Q10(relevance) | 0.60 | 0.40 | 0.59 |
| Q11(completeness) | 0.40 | 0.29 | 0.40 |
| Q12(helpfulness) | 0.59 | 0.41 | 0.61 |

**Table 8. ANOVA F-values between sentence overlap measures and human judgments.**

| Question | Prec. | Rec. | F |
|---|---|---|---|
| Q1(main characters) | 0.60 | 0.61 | 0.58 |
| Q2(location) | 2.58 | 1.94 | 2.36 |
| Q3(time) | 1.11 | 0.67 | 0.97 |
| Q4(readability) | 2.10 | 0.90 | 1.60 |
| Q5(relevance) | 4.55 | 3.75 | 4.28 |
| Q10 (relevance) | 6.33 | 3.46 | 5.15 |
| Q11(completeness) | 3.11 | 4.22 | 3.43 |
| Q12(helpfulness) | 4.53 | 2.54 | 3.72 |

value with 99% confidence, which is 0.57 (the exceptions are highlighted). This suggests that in our case the measurements using sentence overlap as their basis are not correlated with the opinions of subjects about the summaries.

We also performed a one-way ANOVA test using human judgments as independent factors and sentence-overlap based measures as dependent variables. The results are in line with those obtained using Spearman coefficient. They are shown in **Table 8**. The F-values which are statistically significant with 99% confidence are highlighted (the cut-off value for questions Q4-Q12 is 4.89, for Q1 and Q2 – 6.11 and for Q3 – 8.29).

## 4 Conclusions and Future Work

This paper presented an experimental way of evaluating automatically produced summaries of literary short stories.

In the course of our experiments we have remarked a few issues pertinent to evaluating summaries of short fiction. Firstly, higher degree of redundancy of sentences in texts makes measures based on sentence overlap not very enlightening when evaluating extracted summaries. Secondly, at least in our corpus, the sentence overlap-based measures do not correlate well with those measuring opinions of humans about summaries.

This work is exploratory, and as such raises more questions than it answers. In order to evaluate summaries of literary works in a meaningful and reliable way one needs to define criteria which make such summaries suitable or not suitable for a particular purpose. We will explore this issue in our future work. We also intend to apply the pyramid method of evaluating summaries to extracted summaries produced by the human annotators.

## 5 Acknowledgements

The authors would like to express their gratitude to Connexor Oy and especially to Atro Voutilainen for their kind permission to use Connexor Machinese Syntax parser free of charge for research purposes.

## References

J. Bland and D. Altman. 1986. Statistical methods for assessing agreement between two methods of clinical measurement. Lancet. 1986; 1(8476):307-310.

J. Cohen, 1960. A coefficient of agreement for nominal scales. *Educational and Psychological Measurement.* 1960; 20:37-46..

R. Huddleston and G. Pullum. 2002. *The Cambridge Grammar of the English Language Usage*, 123-124. Cambridge University Press.

A. Kazantseva. 2006. *Proc Student Research Workshop* at EACL 2006, 55-63.

I. Mani. 2001. *Automatic Summarization.* John Benjamins B.V.

A. Nenkova and R. Passonneau. 2004. Evaluating content selection in summarization: The pyramid method. *Proc Human Language Technology Conference and NAACL.*

J. Quinlan. 1992. *C4.5: Programs for Machine Learning*, Morgan Kaufmann Pub., San Mateo, CA.

P. Shrout and J. Fleiss. Intraclass correlations: uses in assessing rater reliability. *Psychological Bulletin* 1979; 86:420–428

J. Sim and C. Wright. 2005. The Kappa Statistic in Reliability Studies: Use, Interpretation, and Sample Size Requirements. *Physical Therapy*, 2005(85-3): 257-268.

P. Tapanainen and T. Järvinen. 1997. A non-projective dependency parser. *Proc 5th Conference on Applied Natural Language Processing,* 64-71.

H. Van Halteren and S. Teufel. 2003. Examining the consensus between human summaries: initial experiments with factoid analysis. *HLT/NAACL-2003 Workshop on Automatic Summarization,* 57-64.

# Question Pre-Processing in a QA System on Internet Discussion Groups

**Chuan-Jie Lin and Chun-Hung Cho**
Department of Computer Science and Engineering
National Taiwan Ocean University
No 2, Rd Pei-Ning, Keelung 202, Taiwan, R.O.C
cjlin@mail.ntou.edu.tw; futurehero@seed.net.tw

## Abstract

This paper proposes methods to pre-process questions in the postings before a QA system can find answers in a discussion group in the Internet. Pre-processing includes garbage text removal and question segmentation. Garbage keywords are collected and different length thresholds are assigned to them for garbage text identification. Interrogative forms and question types are used to segment questions. The best performance on the test set achieves 92.57% accuracy in garbage text removal and 85.87% accuracy in question segmentation, respectively.

## 1 Introduction

Question answering has been a hot research topic in recent years. Large scale QA evaluation projects (e.g. TREC QA-Track[1], QA@CLEF[2], and NTCIR[3] QAC and CLQA Tracks) are helpful to the developments of question answering.

However, real automatic QA services are not ready in the Internet. One popular way for Internet users to ask questions and get answers is to visit discussion groups, such as Usenet newsgroups[4] or Yahoo! Answers[5]. Each discussion group focuses on one topic so that users can easily find one to post their questions.

There are two ways a user can try to find answers. You can post your question in a related discussion group and wait for other users to provide answers. Some discussion groups provide search toolbars so that you can search your question first to see if there are similar postings asking the same question. In Yahoo! Answers, you can also judge answers offered by other users and mark the best one.

Postings in discussion groups are good materials to develop a FAQ-style QA system in the Internet. By finding questions in the discussion groups similar to a new posting, responses to these questions can provide answers or relevant information.

But without pre-processing, measuring similarity with original texts will arise some problems:

1. Some phrases such as "many thanks" or "help me please" are not part of a question. These kinds of phrases will introduce noise and harm matching performance.

2. Quite often there is more than one question in one posting. If the question which is most similar to the user's question appears in an existed posting together with other different questions, it will get a lower similarity score than the one it is supposed to have because of other questions.

Therefore, inappropriate phrases should be removed and different questions in one posting should be separated before question comparison.

There is no research focusing on this topic. FAQ finders (Lai et al., 2002; Lytinen and Tomuro, 2002; Burke, 1997) are closely related to this topic. However, there are differences between them. First of all, questions in a FAQ set are often written in perfect grammar without

[1] http://trec.nist.gov/data/qa.html
[2] http://clef-qa.itc.it/
[3] http://research.nii.ac.jp/ntcir/index-en.html
[4] Now they can be accessed via Google Groups: http://groups.google.com/
[5] http://answers.yahoo.com/



*Proceedings of the Workshop on Task-Focused Summarization and Question Answering*, pages 16–23,
Sydney, July 2006. ©2006 Association for Computational Linguistics

garbage text. Second, questions are often paired with answers separately. I.e. there is often one question in one QA pair.

There were some research groups who divided questions into segments. Soricut and Brill (2004) chunked questions and used them as queries to search engines. Saquete et al. (2004) focused on decomposition of a complex question into several sub-questions. In this paper, question segmentation is to identify different questions posed in one posting.

## 2 Garbage Text Removal

### 2.1 Garbage Texts

Articles in discussion groups are colloquial. Users often write articles as if they are talking to other users. For this reason, phrases expressing appreciation, begging, or emotions of writers are often seen in the postings. For example:

> 有關 powerpoint 問題 我想請問一下 [1] 該如何把 access 的整個視窗放到簡報上撥放 謝謝 [2]
> (About Powerpoint, I'd like to ask[1], how to put the whole window seen in Access onto a slide? Thank you[2]!)

The phrases "我想請問一下" ("I'd like to ask") and "謝謝" ("Thank you") are unimportant to the question itself.

These phrases often contain content words, not stop words, and thus are hard to be distinguished with the real questions. If these phrases are not removed, it can happen that two questions are judged "similar" because one of these phrases appears in both questions.

A phrase which contributes no information about a question is called ***garbage text*** in this paper and should be removed beforehand in order to reduce noise. The term ***theme text*** is used to refer to the remaining text.

After examining real querying postings, some characteristics of garbage texts are observed:

1. Some words strongly suggest themselves being in a garbage text, such as "thank" in "thank you so much", or "help" in "who can help me".

2. Some words appear in both theme texts and garbage texts, hence ambiguity arises. For example:

   "請教高手" (Any expert please help)
   "快閃高手" (Flash Expert)

   The first phrase is a garbage text, while the second phrase is a product name. The word "expert" suggests an existence of a garbage text but not in all cases.

Because punctuation marks are not reliable in Chinese, we use sentence fragment as the unit to be processed. A ***sentence fragment*** is defined to be a fragment of text segmented by commas, periods, question marks, exclamation marks, or space marks. A space mark can be a boundary of a sentence fragment only when both characters preceding and following the space mark are not the English letters, digits, or punctuation marks.

### 2.2 Strategies to Remove Garbage Texts

Frequent terms seen in garbage texts are collected as ***garbage keywords*** and grouped into classes according to their meanings and usages. Table 1 gives some examples of classes of garbage keywords collected from the training set.

| Class | Garbage Keywords |
|---|---|
| Please | 請問一下, 煩請,不好意思… |
| Thanks | 感謝,謝謝,感恩,感溫… |
| Help | 賜教,請教,幫我解答,救我… |
| Urgent | 緊急,緊迫,急迫,急… |

**Table 1. Some Classes of Garbage Keywords**

To handle ambiguity, this paper proposes a length information strategy to determine garbage texts as follows:

If a sentence fragment contains a garbage keyword and the length of the fragment after removing the garbage keyword is less than a threshold, the whole fragment will be judged as a garbage text. Otherwise, only the garbage keyword itself is judged as garbage text if it is never in an ambiguous case.

Different length thresholds are assigned to different classes of garbage keywords. If more than one garbage keyword occurring in a fragment, discard all the keywords first, and then compare the length of the remaining fragment with the maximal threshold among the ones corresponding to these garbage keywords.

In order to increase the coverage of garbage keywords, other linguistic resources are used to expand the list of garbage keywords. Synonyms in Tongyici Cilin (同義詞詞林), a thesaurus of Chinese words, are added into the list. More garbage keywords are added by common knowledge.

## 3 Question Segmentation

When a user posts an article in a discussion group, he may pose more than one question at one time. For example, in the following posting:

> Office 2003 和 XP←有何不同之處呢? 哪一個比較新呢? 最新的版本是???????????
> (Office 2003 and XP ← What are the differences between them? Which version is newer? What is the latest version???????????)

there are 3 questions submitted at a time. If a new user wants to know the latest version of Office, responses to the previous posting will give answers.

Table 2 lists the statistics of number of questions in the training set. The first column is the number of questions in one posting. The second and the third columns are the number and the percentage of postings which contain such number of questions, respectively.

| Q# | Post# | Perc (%) |
|---|---|---|
| 1 | 494 | 56.98 |
| 2 | 259 | 29.87 |
| 3 | 82 | 9.46 |
| 4 | 22 | 2.54 |
| 5 | 4 | 0.46 |
| ≥ 6 | 6 | 0.69 |
| **≥ 2** | **373** | **43.02** |
| Total | 867 | 100.00 |

**Table 2. Statistics of Number of Questions in Postings**

As we can see in Table 2, nearly half (43.02%) of the postings contain two or more questions. That is why question segmentation is necessary.

### 3.1 Characteristics of Questions in a Posting

Several characteristics of question texts in postings were found in real discussion groups:

1. Some people use '?' (question mark) at the end of a question while some people do not. In Chinese, some people even separate sentences only by spaces instead of punctuation marks. (Note that there is no space mark between words in Chinese text.)
2. Questions are usually in interrogative form. Either interrogatives or question marks appear in the questions.
3. One question may occur repeatedly in the same posting. It is often the case that a question appears both in the title and in the content. Sometimes a user repeats a sentence several times to show his anxiety.
4. One question may be expressed in different ways in the same posting. The sentences may be similar. For example:

   A: Office2000的剪貼簿只能<u>維持</u>12個項目?
   B: Office2000的剪貼簿只能<u>保持</u>12個項目?
   (Can the clipboard of Office2000 only <u>keep</u> 12 items?)

   "維持" and "保持" are synonyms in the meaning of "keep".

   Dissimilar sentences may also refer to the same question. For example,

   (1) How to use automatic text wrapping in Excel?
   (2) If I want to put two or more lines in one cell, what can I do?
   (3) How to use it?

   These three sentences ask the same question: "How to use automatic text wrapping in Excel?" The second sentence makes a detailed description of what he wants to do. Topic of the third sentence is the same as the first sentence hence is omitted. Topic ellipsis is quite often seen in Chinese.
5. Some users will give examples to explain the questions. These sentences often start with phrases like "for example" or "such as".

### 3.2 Strategies to Separate Questions

According to the observations in Section 3.1, several strategies are proposed to separate questions:

**(1) Separating by Question Mark ('?')**

It is the simplest method. We use it as a baseline strategy.

**(2) Identifying Questions by Interrogative Forms**

Questions are usually in ***interrogative forms*** including subject inversion ("is he…", "does it…"), using interrogatives ("who is…"), or a declarative sentence attached with a question mark ("Office2000 is better?"). Only the third form requires a question mark. The first two forms can specify themselves as questions by text only. Moreover, there are particles in Chinese indicating a question as well, such as "嗎" or "呢".

If a sentence fragment is in interrogative form, it will be judged as a question and separated from the others. A fragment not in interrogative form is merged with the nearest question fragment preceding it (or following it if no preceding one). Note that garbage texts have been removed before question separation.

**(3) Merging or Removing Similar Sentences**

If two sentence fragments are exactly the same, one of them will be removed. If two sentence fragments are similar, they are merged into one question fragment.

Similarity is measured by the Dice coefficient (Dice, 1945) using weights of common words in the two sentence fragments. The similarity of two sentence fragments *X* and *Y* is defined as follows:

$$Sim(X,Y)=\frac{2\times \sum_{k\in X\cap Y} Wt(k)}{\sum_{w\in X} Wt(w)+\sum_{t\in Y} Wt(t)} \quad (1)$$

where $Wt(w)$ is the weight of a word $w$. In Equation 1, $k$ is one of the words appearing in both $X$ and $Y$. Fragments with similarity higher than a threshold are merged together.

The weight of a word is designed as the weight of its part-of-speech as listed in Table 3. Nouns and verbs have higher weights, while adverbs and particles have lower weights. Note that foreign words are assigned a rather high weight, because names of software products such as "Office" or "Oracle" are often written in English, which are foreign words with respect to Chinese.

| POS | Weight |
|---|---|
| Vt (Transitive Verb), FW (Foreign Word) | 100 |
| N (Noun) | 90 |
| Vi (Intransitive Verb) | 80 |
| A (Adjective) | 40 |
| ADV (Adverb), ASP (Tense), C (Connective), DET (Determiner), P (Preposition), T (Particle) | 0 |

**Table 3. Weights of Part-of-Speeches**

Before computing similarity, word segmentation is performed to identify words in Chinese text. After that, a part-of-speech tagger is used to obtain POS information of each word.

**(4) Merging Questions with the Same Type**

The information of question type has been widely adopted in QA systems (Zhang and Lee, 2003; Hovy et al., 2002; Harabagiu et al., 2001). ***Question type*** often refers to the possible type of its answer, such as a person name, a location name, or a temporal expression. The question types used in this paper are PERSON, LOCATION, REASON, QUANTITY, TEMPORAL, COMPARISON, DEFINITION, METHOD, SELECTION, YESNO, and OTHER. Rules to determine question types are created manually.

This strategy tries to merge two question fragments of the same question type. This paper proposes two features to determine the threshold to merge two question fragments: length and sum of term weights of a fragment. Length is measured in characters and term weights are designed as in Table 3.

Merging algorithm is as follows: if the feature value of a question fragment is smaller than a threshold, it will be merged into the preceding question fragment (or the following fragment if no preceding one). This strategy applies recursively until no question fragment has a feature value lower than the threshold.

**(5) Merging Example Fragments**

If a fragment starts with a phrase such as "for example" or "such as", it will be merged into its preceding question fragment.

## 4 Experiments

### 4.1 Experimental Data

All the experimental data were collected from Yahoo! Knowledge+ (Yahoo! 奇摩知識+)[6], discussion groups similar to Yahoo! Answers but using Chinese instead of English.

Three discussion groups, "Business Application" (商務應用), "Website Building" (網站架設), and "Image Processing" (影像處理), were selected to collect querying postings. The reason that we chose these three discussion groups was their moderate growing rates. We could collect enough amount of querying postings published in the same period of time.

The following kinds of postings were not selected as our experimental data:

1. No questions inside
2. Full of algorithms or program codes
3. Full of emoticons or Martian texts (火星文, a funny term used in Chinese to refer to a writing style that uses words with similar pronunciation to replace the original text)
4. Redundant postings

Totally 598 querying postings were collected as the training set and 269 postings as the test set. The real numbers of postings collected from each group are listed in Table 4, where "BA", "WB", and "IP" stand for "Business Application", "Website Building", and "Image Processing", respectively.

| Group | BA | WB | IP |
|---|---|---|---|
| Training Set | 198 | 207 | 193 |
| Test Set | 101 | 69 | 99 |

**Table 4. Numbers of Postings in the Data Set**

Two persons were asked to mark garbage texts and separate questions in the whole data set. If a conflicting case occurred, a third person (who was one of the authors of this paper) would solve the inconsistency.

### 4.2 Garbage Texts Removal

The first factor examined in garbage text removal is the length threshold. Table 5 lists the experimental results on the training set and Table 6 on the test set. All garbage keywords are collected from the training set.

Eight experiments were conducted to use different values as length thresholds. The strategy *Len*k sets the length threshold to be *k* characters (no matter in Chinese or English). Hence, *Len*0 is one baseline strategy which removes only the garbage keyword itself. *LenS* is the other baseline strategy which removes the whole sentence fragment where a garbage keyword appears.

The strategy *Heu* uses different length thresholds for different classes of garbage keywords. The thresholds are heuristic values after observing many examples in the training set.

Accuracy is defined as the percentage of successful removal. In one posting, if all real garbage texts are correctly removed and no other text is wrongly deleted, it counts one successful removal.

| Strategy | Accuracy (%) |
|---|---|
| Len0 | 64.21 |
| LenS | 27.59 |
| Len1 | 73.91 |
| Len2 | 78.43 |
| Len3 | 80.60 |
| Len4 | 78.26 |
| Len5 | 71.91 |
| **Heu** | **99.67** |
| **HeuExp** | **99.67** |

**Table 5. Accuracy of Garbage Text Removal with Different Length Thresholds (Training)**

| Strategy | Accuracy (%) |
|---|---|
| Len0 | 62.08 |
| LenS | 24.54 |
| Len1 | 69.52 |
| Len2 | 75.09 |
| Len3 | 75.46 |
| Len4 | 71.75 |
| Len5 | 65.80 |
| Heu | 87.73 |
| **HeuExp** | **92.57** |

**Table 6. Accuracy of Garbage Text Removal with Different Length Thresholds (Test Set)**

As we can see in both tables, the two baseline strategies are poorer than any other strategy. It means that length threshold is useful to decide garbage existence.

*Heu* is the best strategy (99.67% on the training set and 87.73% on the test set). *Len*3 is

[6] http://tw.knowledge.yahoo.com/

the best strategy (80.60% on the training set and 75.49% on the test set) among *Lenk*, but it is far worse than *Heu*. We can conclude that the length threshold should be assigned individually for each class of garbage words. If it is assigned carefully, the performance of garbage removal will be good.

The second factor is the expansion of garbage keywords. The strategy *HeuExp* is the same as *Heu* except that the list of garbage keywords was expanded as described in Section 2.2.

Comparing the last two rows in Table 6, *HeuExp* strategy improves the performance from 87.73% to 92.57%. It shows that a small amount of postings can provide good coverage of garbage keywords after keyword expansion by using available linguistic resources.

The results of *HeuExp* and *Heu* on the training set are the same. It makes sense because the expanded list suggests garbage existence in the training set no more than the original list does.

### 4.3 Question Segmentation

**Overall Strategies**

Six experiments were conducted to see the performance of different strategies for question segmentation. The strategies used in each experiment are:

*Baseline*: using only '?' (question mark) to separate questions

*SameS*: removing repeated sentence fragments then separating by '?'

*Interrg*: after removing repeated sentence fragments, separating questions which are in interrogative forms

*SimlrS*: following the strategy *Interrg*, removing or merging similar sentence fragments of the same question type

*ForInst*: following the strategy *SimlrS*, merging a sentence fragment beginning with "for instance" and alike with its preceding question fragment

*SameQT*: following the strategy *ForInst*, merging question fragments of the same question type without considering similarity

Table 7 and Table 8 depict the results of the six experiments on the training set and the test set, respectively. The second column in each table lists the accuracy which is defined as the *percentage* of postings which are separated into the same number of questions as manually tagged. The third column gives the *number* of postings which are correctly separated. The fourth and the fifth columns contain the numbers of postings which are separated into more and fewer questions, respectively.

| Strategy | Acc (%) | Same | More | Fewer |
|---|---|---|---|---|
| Baseline | 50.67 | 303 | 213 | 82 |
| SameS | 59.03 | 353 | 156 | 89 |
| Interrg | 64.88 | 388 | 204 | 6 |
| SimlrS | 75.08 | 449 | 141 | 8 |
| ForInst | 75.75 | 453 | 137 | 8 |
| **SameQT** | **88.29** | 528 | 13 | 57 |

**Table 7. Accuracy of Question Segmentation by Different Strategies (Training Set)**

| Strategy | Acc (%) | Same | More | Fewer |
|---|---|---|---|---|
| Baseline | 54.28 | 146 | 84 | 39 |
| SameS | 65.43 | 176 | 54 | 39 |
| Interrg | 65.43 | 176 | 93 | 0 |
| SimlrS | 74.35 | 200 | 68 | 1 |
| ForInst | 74.35 | 200 | 68 | 1 |
| **SameQT** | **85.87** | 231 | 16 | 22 |

**Table 8. Accuracy of Question Segmentation by Different Strategies (Test Set)**

As we can see in Table 7, performance is improved gradually after adding new strategies. *SameQT* achieves the best performance with 88.29% accuracy. Same conclusion could also be made by the results on the test set. *SameQT* is the best one with 85.87% accuracy.

In Table 7, *Baseline* achieves only 50.67% accuracy. That matches our observations: (1) one question is often stated many times by sentences ended with question marks in one posting (as 213 postings were separated into more questions); (2) some users do not use '?' in writing (as 82 postings were separated into fewer questions).

*SameS* greatly reduces the cases (57 postings) of separation into more questions by removing repeated sentences.

On the other hand, *Interrg* greatly reduces the cases (76 postings) of separation into fewer questions. Many question sentences without question marks were successfully captured by detecting the interrogative forms.

*SimlrS* also improves a lot (successfully reducing number of questions separated in 63 postings). But *ForInst* only improves a little. It is more common to express one question several times in different way than giving examples.

*SameQT* achieves the best performance, which means that question type is a good strategy. Different ways to express a question are usually in the same question type. Comparing with *SimlrS* which also considers sentence fragments in the same question type, more improvement comes from the successful merging of fragments with topic ellipses, co-references, or paraphrases. However, there may be other questions in the same question type which are wrongly merged together (as 49 failures in the training set).

Considering the results on the test set, *Interrg* does not improve the overall performance comparing to *SameS* because the improvement equals the drop. *ForInst* does not improve either. It seems that giving examples is not common in the discussion groups.

**Thresholds in *SameQT***

In the strategy *SameQT*, two features, length and sum of term weights, are used to determine thresholds to merge question fragments as mentioned in Section 3.2. In order to decide which feature is better and which threshold value should be set, two experiments were conducted.

| LenThr | Acc (%) | LenThr | Acc (%) |
|---|---|---|---|
| 0 | 75.75 | 9 | 85.62 |
| 3 | 76.25 | 10 | 86.62 |
| 4 | 78.60 | 15 | 88.29 |
| 5 | 81.94 | 20 | 88.13 |
| 6 | 84.95 | **30** | **88.63** |
| 7 | 85.79 | 40 | 88.29 |
| 8 | 86.29 | ∞ | **88.29** |

**Table 9. Accuracy of Question Segmentation with Different Length Thresholds**

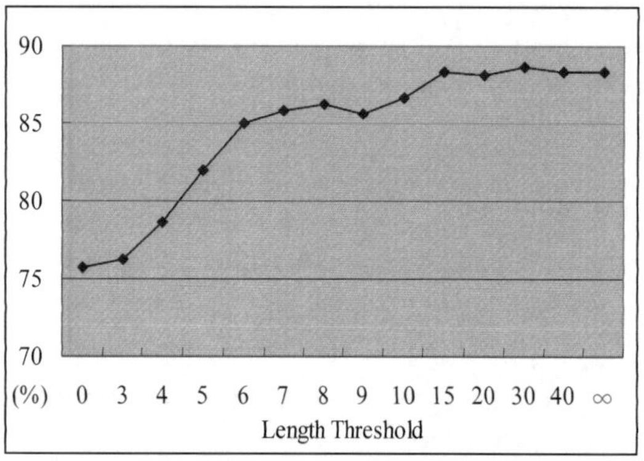


**Figure 1. Accuracy of Question Segmentation with Different Length Thresholds**

Table 9 depicts the experimental results of using length of sentence fragments as merging threshold. The column "LenThr" lists different settings of length threshold and the column "Acc" gives the accuracy.

The performance is gradually improved as the value of length threshold increases. The best one is LenThr=30 with 88.63% accuracy. However, "Always Merging" (LenThr=∞) achieves 88.29% accuracy, which is also acceptable comparing to the best performance. Fig 1 shows the curve of accuracy against length threshold.

Table 10 presents the experimental results of using sum of term weights as merging thresold. The column "WgtThr" lists different settings of length threshold and the column "Acc" gives the accuracy.

The performance is also gradually improved as the value of weight threshold increases. When WgtThr is set to be 500, 700, or 900, the performance is the best, with 88.46% accuracy. But the same as the threshold settings of length feature, the best one does not outperform "Always Merging" strategy (WgtThr=∞, 88.29% accuracy) too much. Fig 2 shows the curve of accuracy against similarity threshold.

| WgtThr | Acc (%) | WgtThr | Acc (%) |
|---|---|---|---|
| 0 | 75.75 | 350 | 87.29 |
| 50 | 77.93 | 400 | 88.13 |
| 100 | 83.11 | 450 | 88.29 |
| 150 | 85.28 | **500** | **88.46** |
| 200 | 86.29 | **700** | **88.46** |
| 250 | 86.79 | **900** | **88.46** |
| 300 | 87.46 | ∞ | **88.29** |

**Table 10. Accuracy of Question Segmentation with Different Weight Thresholds**

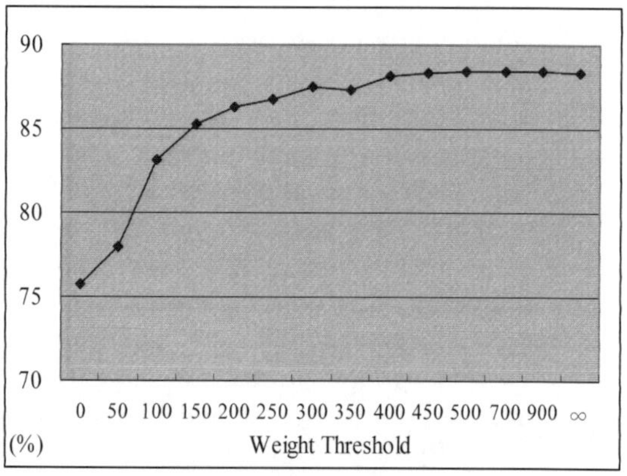


**Figure 2. Accuracy of Question Segmentation with Different Weight Thresholds**

From the results of above experiments, we can see that although using length feature with a threshold LenThr=30 achieves the best performance, "Always Merging" is more welcome for a online system because no feature extraction or computation is needed with only a little sacrifice of performance. Hence we choose "Always Merging" as merging strategy in *SameQT*.

## 5 Conclusion and Future Work

This paper proposes question pre-processing methods for a FQA-style QA system on discussion groups in the Internet. For a posting already existing or being submitted to a discussion group, garbage texts in it are removed first, and then different questions in it are identified so that they can be compared with other questions individually.

An expanded list of garbage keywords is used to detect garbage texts. If there is a garbage keyword appearing in a sentence fragment and the fragment has a length shorter than a threshold corresponding to the class of the garbage keyword, the fragment will be judged as a garbage text. This method achieves 92.57% accuracy on the test set. It means that a small set is sufficient to collect all classes of garbage keywords.

In question segmentation, sentence fragments in interrogative forms are considered as question fragments. Besides, repeated fragments are removed and fragments of the same question types are merged into one fragment. The overall accuracy is 85.87% on the test set.

In the future, performance of a QA system with or without question pre-processing will be evaluated to verify its value.

New methods to create the list of garbage keywords more robotically should be studied, as well as the automatic assignments of the length thresholds of classes of garbage keywords.

New feature should be discovered in the future in order to segment questions more accurately.

Although the strategies and the thresholds are developed according to experimental data in Chinese, we can see that many of them are language-independent or can be adapted with not too much effort.

## Reference


Burke, Robin, Kristian Hammond, Vladimir Kulyukin, Steven Lytinen, Noriko Tomuro, and Scott Schoenberg (1997) "Natural language processing in the FAQFinder system: Results and prospects," *Proceedings of the 1997 AAAI Spring Symposium on Natural Language Processing for the World Wide Web*, pp. 17-26.

Dice, Lee R. (1945) "Measures of the amount of ecologic association between species," *Journal of Ecology*, Vol. 26, pp. 297-302.

Harabagiu, Sanda, Dan Moldovan, Marius Paşca, Rada Mihalcea, Mihai Surdeanu, Răzvan Bunescu, Roxana Gîrju, Vasile Rus, and Paul Morărescu (2001) "The Role of Lexico-Semantic Feedback in Open-Domain Textual Question-Answering," *Proceedings of ACL-EACL 2001*, pp. 274-281.

Hovy, Eduard, Ulf Hermjakob, and Chin-Yew Lin (2002) "The Use of External Knowledge in Factoid QA," *Proceedings of TREC-10*, pp. 644-652.

Lai, Yu-Sheng, Kuao-Ann Fung, and Chung-Hsien Wu (2002) "FAQ Mining via List Detection," *Proceedings of the COLING Workshop on Multilingual Summarization and Question Answering*.

Lytinen, Steven and Noriko Tomuro (2002) "The use of question types to match questions in FAQFinder," *Proceedings of the 2002 AAAI Spring Symposium on Mining Answers from Texts and Knowledge Bases*, pp. 46-53.

Saquete, Estela, Patricio Martinez-Barco, Rafael Munoz, and Jose Luis Vicedo Gonzalez (2004) "Splitting Complex Temporal Questions for Question Answering Systems," *Proceedings of ACL 2004*, pp. 566-573.

Soricut, Radu and Eric Brill (2004) "Automatic Question Answering: Beyond the Factoid," *Proceedings of HLT-NAACL 2004*, pp. 57-64.

Zhang, Dell and Wee Sun Lee (2003) "Question Classification using Support Vector Machines," *Proceedings of SIGIR 2003*, pp. 26-32.

# Situated Question Answering in the Clinical Domain: Selecting the Best Drug Treatment for Diseases

**Dina Demner-Fushman**[1,3] **and Jimmy Lin**[1,2,3]
[1]Department of Computer Science
[2]College of Information Studies
[3]Institute for Advanced Computer Studies
University of Maryland
College Park, MD 20742, USA
demner@cs.umd.edu, jimmylin@umd.edu

## Abstract

Unlike open-domain factoid questions, clinical information needs arise within the rich context of patient treatment. This environment establishes a number of constraints on the design of systems aimed at physicians in real-world settings. In this paper, we describe a clinical question answering system that focuses on a class of commonly-occurring questions: "What is the best drug treatment for *X*?", where *X* can be any disease. To evaluate our system, we built a test collection consisting of thirty randomly-selected diseases from an existing secondary source. Both an automatic and a manual evaluation demonstrate that our system compares favorably to PubMed, the search system most commonly-used by physicians today.

## 1 Introduction

Over the past several years, question answering (QA) has emerged as a general framework for addressing users' information needs. Instead of returning "hits", as information retrieval systems do, QA systems respond to natural language questions with concise, targeted information. Recently, research focus has shifted away from so-called factoid questions such as "What are pennies made of?" and "What country is Aswan High Dam located in?" to more complex questions such as "How have South American drug cartels been using banks in Liechtenstein to launder money?" and "What was the Pentagon panel's position with respect to the dispute over the US Navy training range on the island of Vieques?"—so-called "relationship" and "opinion" questions, respectively.

These complex information needs differ from factoid questions in many important ways. Unlike factoids, they cannot be answered by named-entities and other short noun phrases. They do not occur in isolation, but are rather embedded within a broader context, i.e., a "scenario". These complex questions set forth parameters of the desired knowledge, which may include additional facts about the motivation of the information seeker, her assumptions, her current state of knowledge, etc. Presently, most systems that attempt to tackle such complex questions are aimed at serving intelligence analysts, for activities such as counter-terrorism and war-fighting.

Systems for addressing complex information needs are interesting because they provide an opportunity to explore the role of semantic structures in question answering, e.g., (Narayanan and Harabagiu, 2004). Opportunities include explicit semantic representations for capturing the content of questions and documents, deep inferential mechanisms (Moldovan et al., 2002), and attempts to model task-specific influences in information-seeking environments (Freund et al., 2005).

Our own interest in question answering falls in line with these recent developments, but we focus on a different type of user—the primary care physician. The need to answer questions related to patient care at the point of service has been well studied and documented (Gorman et al., 1994; Ely et al., 1999; Ely et al., 2005). However, research has shown that existing search systems, e.g., PubMed, are often unable to supply clinically-relevant answers in a timely manner (Gorman et al., 1994; Chambliss and Conley, 1996). Clinical question answering represents a high-impact application that has the potential to improve the quality of medical care.



*Proceedings of the Workshop on Task-Focused Summarization and Question Answering*, pages 24–31,
Sydney, July 2006. 

From a research perspective, the clinical domain is attractive because substantial medical knowledge has already been codified in the Unified Medical Language System (UMLS) (Lindberg et al., 1993). This large ontology enables us to explore knowledge-rich techniques and move beyond question answering methods primarily driven by keyword matching. In this work, we describe a paradigm of medical practice known as evidence-based medicine and explain how it can be computationally captured in a semantic domain model. Two separate evaluations demonstrate that semantic modeling yields gains in question answering performance.

## 2 Considerations for Clinical QA

We begin our exploration of clinical question answering by first discussing design constraints imposed by the domain and the information-seeking environment. The practice of evidence-based medicine (EBM) provides a well-defined process model for situating our system. EBM is a widely-accepted paradigm for medical practice that involves the explicit use of current best evidence, i.e., high-quality patient-centered clinical research reported in the primary medical literature, to make decisions about patient care. As shown by previous work (De Groote and Dorsch, 2003), citations from the MEDLINE database maintained by the National Library of Medicine serve as a good source of evidence.

Thus, we conceive of clinical question answering systems as fulfilling a decision-support role by retrieving highly-relevant MEDLINE abstracts in response to a clinical question. This represents a departure from previous systems, which focus on extracting short text segments from larger sources. The implications of making potentially life-altering decisions mean that all evidence must be carefully examined in context. For example, the efficacy of a drug in treating a disease is always framed in the context of a specific study on a sample population, over a set duration, at some fixed dosage, etc. The physician simply cannot recommend a particular course of action without considering all these complex factors. Thus, an "answer" without adequate support is not useful. Given that a MEDLINE abstract—on the order of 250 words, equivalent to a long paragraph—generally encapsulates the context of a clinical study, it serves as a logical answer unit and an entry point to the information necessary to answer the physician's question (e.g., via drill-down to full text articles).

In order for a clinical QA system to be successful, it must be suitably integrated into the daily activities of a physician. Within a clinic or a hospital setting, the traditional desktop application is not the most ideal interface for a retrieval system. In most cases, decisions about patient care must be made by the bedside. Thus, a PDA is an ideal vehicle for delivering question answering capabilities (Hauser et al., 2004). However, the form factor and small screen size of such devices places constraints on system design. In particular, since the physician is unable to view large amounts of text, precision is of utmost importance.

In summary, this section outlines considerations for question answering in the clinical domain: the necessity of contextualized answers, the rationale for adopting MEDLINE abstract as the response unit, and the importance of high precision.

## 3 EBM and Clinical QA

Evidence-based medicine not only supplies a process model for situating question answering capabilities, but also provides a framework for codifying the knowledge involved in retrieving answers. This section describes how the EBM paradigm provides the basis of the semantic domain model for our question answering system.

Evidence-based medicine offers three facets of the clinical domain, that, when taken together, describe a model for addressing complex clinical information needs. The first facet, shown in Table 1 (left column), describes the four main tasks that physicians engage in. The second facet pertains to the structure of a well-built clinical question. Richardson et al. (1995) identify four key elements, as shown in Table 1 (middle column). These four elements are often referenced with a mnemonic PICO, which stands for Patient/Problem, Intervention, Comparison, and Outcome. Finally, the third facet serves as a tool for appraising the strength of evidence, i.e., how much confidence should a physician have in the results? For this work, we adopted a system with three levels of recommendations, as shown in Table 1 (right column).

By integrating these three perspectives of evidence-based medicine, we conceptualize clinical question answering as "semantic unification" between information needs expressed in a

| Clinical Tasks | PICO Elements | Strength of Evidence |
|---|---|---|
| **Therapy:** Selecting effective treatments for patients, taking into account other factors such as risk and cost.<br><br>**Diagnosis:** Selecting and interpreting diagnostic tests, while considering their precision, accuracy, acceptability, cost, and safety.<br><br>**Prognosis:** Estimating the patient's likely course with time and anticipating likely complications.<br><br>**Etiology:** Identifying the causes for a patient's disease. | **Patient/Problem:** What is the primary problem or disease? What are the characteristics of the patient (e.g., age, gender, co-existing conditions, etc.)?<br><br>**Intervention:** What is the main intervention (e.g., diagnostic test, medication, therapeutic procedure, etc.)?<br><br>**Comparison:** What is the main intervention compared to (e.g., no intervention, another drug, another therapeutic procedure, a placebo, etc.)?<br><br>**Outcome:** What is the effect of the intervention (e.g., symptoms relieved or eliminated, cost reduced, etc.)? | **A-level evidence** is based on consistent, good quality patient-oriented evidence presented in systematic reviews, randomized controlled clinical trials, cohort studies, and meta-analyses.<br><br>**B-level evidence** is inconsistent, limited quality patient-oriented evidence in the same types of studies.<br><br>**C-level evidence** is based on disease-oriented evidence or studies less rigorous than randomized controlled clinical trials, cohort studies, systematic reviews and meta-analyses. |

Table 1: The three facets of evidence-based medicine.

PICO-based knowledge structure and corresponding structures extracted from MEDLINE abstracts. Naturally, this matching process should be sensitive to the clinical task and the strength of evidence of the retrieved abstracts. As conceived, clinical question answering is a knowledge-intensive endeavor that requires automatic identification of PICO elements from MEDLINE abstracts.

Ideally, a clinical question answering system should be capable of directly performing this semantic match on abstracts, but the size of the MEDLINE database (over 16 million citations) makes this approach currently unfeasible. As an alternative, we rely on PubMed,[1] a boolean search engine provided by the National Library of Medicine, to retrieve an initial set of results that we then postprocess in greater detail—this is the standard two-stage architecture commonly-employed by many question answering systems (Hirschman and Gaizauskas, 2001).

The complete architecture of our system is shown in Figure 1. The query formulation module converts the clinical question into a PubMed search query, identifies the clinical task, and extracts the appropriate PICO elements. PubMed returns an initial list of MEDLINE citations, which is analyzed by the knowledge extractor to identify clinically-relevant elements. These elements serve as input to the semantic matcher, and are compared to corresponding elements extracted from the question. Citations are then scored and the top ranking ones are returned as answers.

[1] `http://www.ncbi.nih.gov/entrez/`

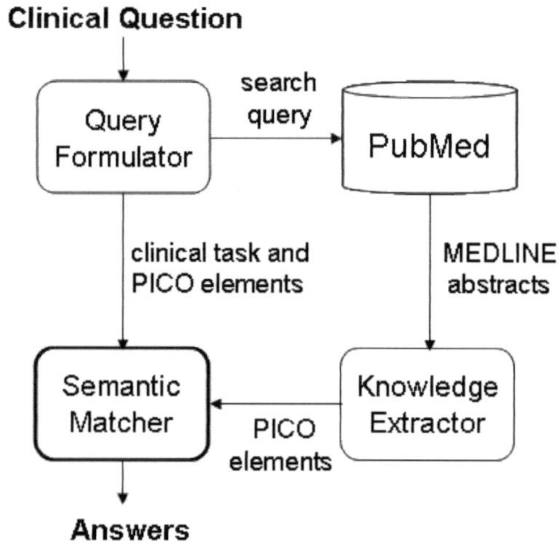


Figure 1: Architecture of our clinical question answering system.

Although we have outlined a general framework for clinical question answering, the space of all possible patient care questions is immense, and attempts to develop a comprehensive system is beyond the scope of this paper. Instead, we focus on a subset of therapy questions: specifically, questions of the form "What is the best drug treatment for *X*?", where *X* can be any disease. We have chosen to tackle this class of questions because studies of physicians' question-asking behavior in natural settings have revealed that this question type occurs frequently (Ely et al., 1999). By leveraging the natural distribution of clinical questions, we can make the greatest impact with the least amount of development effort. For this class of questions, we have implemented a working system with the architecture described in Figure 1. The next three sections detail each module.

## 4 Query Formulator

Since our system only handles one question type, the query formulator is relatively simple: the task is known in advance to be therapy and the Problem PICO element is the disease asked about in the clinical question. In order to facilitate the semantic matching process, we employ MetaMap (Aronson, 2001) to identify the concept in the UMLS ontology that corresponds to the disease; UMLS also provides alternative names and other expansions.

The query formulator also generates a query to PubMed, the National Library of Medicine's boolean search engine for MEDLINE. As an example, the following query is issued to retrieve hits for the disease "meningitis":

> (Meningitis[mh:noexp]) AND drug therapy[sh] AND hasabstract[text] AND Clinical Trial[pt] AND English[Lang] AND humans[mh] AND (1900[PDAT] : 2003/03[PDAT])

In order to get the best possible set of initial citations, we employ MeSH (Medical Subject Headings) terms when available. MeSH terms are controlled vocabulary concepts assigned manually by trained medical librarians in the indexing process (based on the full text of the article), and encode a substantial amount of knowledge about the contents of the citation. PubMed allows searches on MeSH headings, which usually yield highly accurate results. In addition, we limit retrieved citations to those that have the MeSH heading "drug therapy"and those that describe a clinical trial (another metadata field). By default, PubMed orders citations chronologically in reverse.

## 5 Knowledge Extractor

The knowledge extraction module provides the basic frame elements used in the semantic matching process, described in the next section. We employ previously-implemented components (Demner-Fushman and Lin, 2005) that identify PICO elements within a MEDLINE citation using a combination of knowledge-based and statistical machine-learning techniques. Of the four PICO elements prescribed by evidence-based medicine practitioners, only the Problem and Outcome elements are relevant for this application (there are no Interventions and Comparisons for our question type). The Problem is the main disease under consideration in an abstract, and outcomes are statements that assert clinical findings, e.g., efficacy of a drug or a comparison between two drugs. The ability to precisely identify these clinically-relevant elements provides the foundation for semantic question answering capabilities.

## 6 Semantic Matcher

Evidence-based medicine identifies three different sets of factors that must be taken into account when assessing citation relevance. These considerations are computationally operationalized in the semantic matcher, which takes as input elements identified by the knowledge extractor and scores the relevance of each PubMed citation with respect to the question. After matching, the top-scoring abstracts are presented to the physician as answers. The individual score of a citation is comprised of three components:

$$S_{\text{EBM}} = S_{\text{PICO}} + S_{\text{SoE}} + S_{\text{MeSH}} \qquad (1)$$

By codifying the principles of evidence-based medicine, our semantic matcher attempts to satisfy information needs through conceptual analysis, as opposed to simple keyword matching. In the following subsections, we describe each of these components in detail.

### 6.1 PICO Matching

The score of an abstract based on PICO elements, $S_{\text{PICO}}$, is broken up into two separate scores:

$$S_{\text{PICO}} = S_{\text{problem}} + S_{\text{outcome}} \qquad (2)$$

The first component in the above equation, $S_{\text{problem}}$, reflects a match between the primary problem in the query frame and the primary problem identified in the abstract. A score of 1 is given if the problems match exactly, based on their unique UMLS concept id (as provided by MetaMap). Matching based on concept ids addresses the issue of terminological variation. Failing an exact match of concept ids, a partial string match is given a score of $0.5$. If the primary problem in the query has no overlap with the primary problem from the abstract, a score of $-1$ is given.

The outcome-based score $S_{\text{outcome}}$ is the value assigned to the highest-scoring outcome sentence, as determined by the knowledge extractor. Since the desired outcome (i.e., improve the patient's condition) is implicit in the clinical question, our system only considers the inherent quality of outcome statements in the abstract. Given a match on the primary problem, most clinical outcomes are likely to be of interest to the physician.

For the drug treatment scenario, there is no intervention or comparison, and so these elements do not contribute to the semantic matching.

### 6.2 Strength of Evidence

The relevance score of a citation based on the strength of evidence is calculated as follows:

$$S_{\text{SoE}} = S_{\text{journal}} + S_{\text{study}} + S_{\text{date}} \quad (3)$$

Citations published in core and high-impact journals such as Journal of the American Medical Association (JAMA) get a score of $0.6$ for $S_{\text{journal}}$, and $0$ otherwise. In terms of the study type, $S_{\text{study}}$, clinical trials receive a score of $0.5$; observational studies, $0.3$; all non-clinical publications, $-1.5$; and $0$ otherwise. The study type is directly encoded as metadata in a MEDLINE citation.

Finally, recency factors into the strength of evidence score according to the formula below:

$$S_{\text{date}} = (year_{\text{publication}} - year_{\text{current}})/100 \quad (4)$$

A mild penalty decreases the score of a citation proportionally to the time difference between the date of the search and the date of publication.

### 6.3 MeSH Matching

The final component of the EBM score reflects task-specific considerations, and is computed from MeSH terms associated with each citation:

$$S_{\text{MeSH}} = \sum_{t \in \text{MeSH}} \alpha(t) \quad (5)$$

The function $\alpha(t)$ maps MeSH terms to positive scores for positive indicators, negative scores for negative indicators, or zero otherwise.

Negative indicators include MeSH headings associated with genomics, such as "genetics" and "cell physiology". Positive indicators for therapy were derived from the clinical query filters used in PubMed searches (Haynes et al., 1994); examples include "drug administration routes" and any of its children in the MeSH hierarchy. A score of $\pm 1$ is given if the MeSH descriptor or qualifier is marked as the main theme of the article (indicated via the star notation by indexers), and $\pm 0.5$ otherwise.

## 7 Evaluation Methodology

*Clinical Evidence (CE)* is a periodic report created by the British Medical Journal (BMJ) Publishing Group that summarizes the best treatments for a few dozen diseases at the time of publication. We were able to mine the June 2004 edition to create a test collection to evaluate our system. Note that the existence of such secondary sources does not obviate the need for clinical question answering because they are perpetually falling out of date due to rapid advances in medicine. Furthermore, such reports are currently created by highly-experienced physicians, which is an expensive and time-consuming process. From *CE*, we randomly extracted thirty diseases, creating a development set of five questions and a test set of twenty-five questions. Some examples include: acute asthma, chronic prostatitis, community acquired pneumonia, and erectile dysfunction.

We conducted two evaluations—one automatic and one manual—that compare the original PubMed hits and the output of our semantic matcher. The first evaluation is based on ROUGE, a commonly-used summarization metric that computes the unigram overlap between a particular text and one or more reference texts.[2] The treatment overview for each disease in *CE* is accompanied by a number of citations (used in writing the overview itself)—the abstract texts of these cited articles serve as our references. We adopt this approach because medical journals require abstracts that provide factual information summarizing the main points of the studies. We assume that the closer an abstract is to these reference abstracts (as measured by ROUGE-1 precision), the more relevant it is. On average, each disease overview contains $48.4$ citations; however, we were only able to gather abstracts of those that were contained in MEDLINE (34.7 citations per disease, min 8, max 100). For evaluation purposes, we restricted abstracts under consideration to those that were published before our edition of *CE*. To quantify the performance of our system, we computed the average ROUGE score over the top one, three, five, and ten hits of our EBM and baseline systems.

To supplement our automatic evaluation, we also conducted a double-blind manual evaluation

[2] We ran ROUGE-1.5.5 with DUC 2005 settings.

| | PubMed | EBM | PICO | SoE | MeSH |
|---|---|---|---|---|---|
| 1 | 0.160 | 0.205 (+27.7%)$^{\triangle}$ | 0.186 (+16.1%)$^{\circ}$ | 0.192 (+20.0%)$^{\circ}$ | 0.166 (+3.6%)$^{\circ}$ |
| 3 | 0.162 | 0.202 (+24.6%)$^{\blacktriangle}$ | 0.192 (+18.0%)$^{\blacktriangle}$ | 0.204 (+25.5%)$^{\blacktriangle}$ | 0.172 (+6.1%)$^{\circ}$ |
| 5 | 0.166 | 0.198 (+19.5%)$^{\blacktriangle}$ | 0.196 (+18.0%)$^{\blacktriangle}$ | 0.201 (+21.3%)$^{\blacktriangle}$ | 0.168 (+1.2%)$^{\circ}$ |
| 10 | 0.170 | 0.196 (+15.5%)$^{\blacktriangle}$ | 0.191 (+12.5%)$^{\blacktriangle}$ | 0.195 (+15.1%)$^{\blacktriangle}$ | 0.174 (+2.8%)$^{\circ}$ |

Table 2: Results of automatic evaluation: average ROUGE score using cited abstracts in *CE* as references. The EBM column represents performance of our complete domain model. PICO, SoE, and MeSH represent performance of each component. ($^{\circ}$ denotes n.s., $^{\triangle}$ denotes sig. at 0.95, $^{\blacktriangle}$ denotes sig. at 0.99)

| **PubMed results** | **EBM-reranked results** |
|---|---|
| Effect of vitamin A supplementation on childhood morbidity and mortality. | A comparison of ceftriaxone and cefuroxime for the treatment of bacterial meningitis in children. |
| Intrathecal chemotherapy in carcinomatous meningitis from breast cancer. | Randomised comparison of chloramphenicol, ampicillin, cefotaxime, and ceftriaxone for childhood bacterial meningitis. |
| Isolated leptomeningeal carcinomatosis (carcinomatous meningitis) after taxane-induced major remission in patients with advanced breast cancer. | The beneficial effects of early dexamethasone administration in infants and children with bacterial meningitis. |

Table 3: Titles of the top abstracts retrieved in response to the question "What is the best treatment for meningitis?", before and after applying our semantic reranking algorithm.

of the system. The top five citations from both the original PubMed results and the output of our semantic matcher were gathered, blinded, and randomized (see Table 3 for an example of top results obtained by PubMed and our system). The first author of this paper, who is a medical doctor, manually evaluated the abstracts. Since the sources of the abstracts were hidden, judgments were guaranteed to be impartial. All abstracts were evaluated on a four point scale: not relevant, marginally relevant, relevant, and highly relevant, which corresponds to a score of zero to three.

## 8 Results

The results of our automatic evaluation are shown in Table 2: the rows show average ROUGE scores at one, three, five, and ten hits, respectively. In addition to the PubMed baseline and our complete EBM model, we conducted a component-level analysis of our semantic matching algorithm. Three separate ablation studies isolate the effects of the PICO-based score, the strength of evidence score, and the MeSH-based score (columns "PICO", "SoE", and "MeSH").

At all document cutoffs, the quality of the EBM-reranked hits is higher than that of the original PubMed hits, as measured by ROUGE. The differences are statistically significant, according to the Wilcoxon signed-rank test, the standard non-parametric test employed in IR.

Based on the component analysis, we can see that the strength of evidence score is responsible for the largest performance gain, although the combination of all three components outperforms each one individually (for the most part). All three components of our semantic model contribute to the overall QA performance, which is expected because clinical relevance is a multi-faceted property that requires a multitude of considerations. Evidence-based medicine provides a theory of these factors, and we have shown that a question answering algorithm which operationalizes EBM yields good results.

The distribution of human judgments from our manual evaluation is shown in Figure 2. For the development set, the average human judgment of the original PubMed hits is 1.52 (between "marginally relevant" and "relevant"); after semantic matching, 2.32 (better than "relevant"). For the test set, the averages are 1.49 before ranking and 2.10 after semantic matching. These results show that our system performs significantly better than the PubMed baseline.

The performance improvement observed in our experiments is encouraging, considering that we were starting off with a strong state-of-the-art

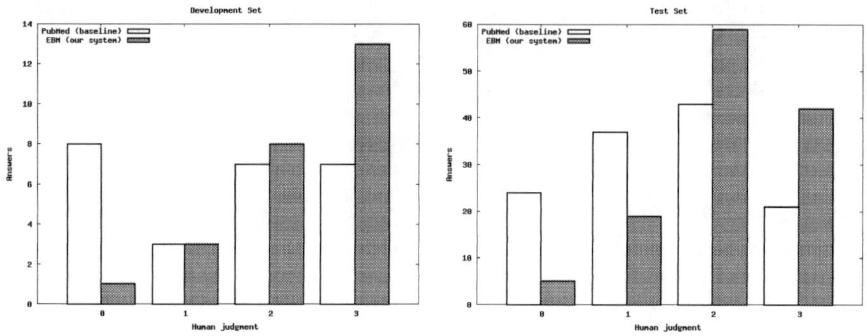


Figure 2: Results of our manual evaluation: distribution of judgments, for development set (left) and test set (right). (0=not relevant, 1=marginally relevant, 2=relevant, 3=highly relevant)

PubMed baseline that leverages MeSH terms. All initial citations retrieved by PubMed were clinical trials and "about" the disease in question, as determined by human indexers. Our work demonstrates that principles of evidence-based medicine can be codified in an algorithm.

Since a number of abstracts were both automatically evaluated with ROUGE and manually assessed, it is possible to determine the degree to which automatic metrics predict human judgments. For the 125 human judgments gathered on the test set, we computed a Pearson's $r$ score of $0.544$, which indicates moderate predictiveness. Due to the structure of our PubMed query, the keyword content of retrieved abstracts are relatively homogeneous. Nevertheless, automatic evaluation with ROUGE appears to be useful.

## 9 Discussion and Related Work

Recently, researchers have become interested in restricted-domain question answering because it provides an opportunity to explore the use of knowledge-rich techniques without having to tackle the commonsense reasoning problem. Knowledge-based techniques dependent on rich semantic representations contrast with TREC-style factoid question answering, which is primarily driven by keyword matching and named-entity detection.

Our work represents a successful case study of how semantic models can be employed to capture domain knowledge (the practice of medicine, in our case). The conception of question answering as the matching of knowledge frames provides us with an opportunity to experiment with semantic representations that capture the content of both documents and information needs. In our case, PICO-based scores were found to have a positive impact on performance. The strength of evidence and the MeSH-based scores represent attempts to model user requirements by leveraging meta-level information not directly present in either questions or candidate answers. Both contribute positively to performance. Overall, the construction of our semantic model is enabled by the UMLS ontology, which provides an enumeration of relevant concepts (e.g., the names of diseases, drugs, etc.) and semantic relations between those concepts.

Question answering in the clinical domain is an emerging area of research that has only recently begun to receive serious attention. As a result, there exist relatively few points of comparison to our own work, as the research space is sparsely populated.

The idea that information systems should be sensitive to the practice of evidence-based medicine is not new. Many researchers have studied MeSH terms associated with basic clinical tasks (Mendonça and Cimino, 2001; Haynes et al., 1994). Although originally developed as a tool to assist in query formulation, Booth (2000) pointed out that PICO frames can be employed to structure IR results for improving precision; PICO-based querying is merely an instance of faceted querying, which has been widely used by librarians since the invention of automated retrieval systems. The feasibility of automatically identifying outcome statements in secondary sources has been demonstrated by Niu and Hirst (2004), but our work differs in its focus on the primary medical literature. Approaching clinical needs from a different perspective, the PERSIVAL system leverages patient records to rerank search results (McKeown et al., 2003). Since the primary focus is on personalization, this work can be viewed as complementary to our own.

The dearth of related work and the lack of a preexisting clinical test collection to a large extent explains the *ad hoc* nature of some aspects of our semantic matching algorithm. All weights were heuristically chosen to reflect our understanding of the domain, and were not optimized in a principled manner. Nevertheless, performance gains observed in the development set carried over to the blind held-out test collection, providing confidence in the generality of our methods. Developing a more formal scoring model for evidence-based medicine will be the subject of future work.

## 10 Conclusion

We see this work as having two separate contributions. From the viewpoint of computational linguistics, we have demonstrated the effectiveness of a knowledge-rich approach to QA based on matching questions with answers at the semantic level. From the viewpoint of medical informatics, we have shown how principles of evidence-based medicine can be operationalized in a system to support physicians. We hope that this work paves the way for future high-impact applications.

## 11 Acknowledgments

This work was supported in part by the National Library of Medicine. The second author wishes to thank Esther and Kiri for their loving support.

## References

A. Aronson. 2001. Effective mapping of biomedical text to the UMLS Metathesaurus: The MetaMap program. In *Proceeding of the AMIA 2001*.

A. Booth. 2000. Formulating the question. In A. Booth and G. Walton, editors, *Managing Knowledge in Health Services*. Facet Publishing.

M. Chambliss and J. Conley. 1996. Answering clinical questions. *The Journal of Family Practice*, 43:140–144.

S. De Groote and J. Dorsch. 2003. Measuring use patterns of online journals and databases. *Journal of the Medical Library Association*, 91(2):231–240, April.

D. Demner-Fushman and J. Lin. 2005. Knowledge extraction for clinical question answering: Preliminary results. In *Proceedings of the AAAI-05 Workshop on Question Answering in Restricted Domains*.

J. Ely, J. Osheroff, M. Ebell, G. Bergus, B. Levy, M. Chambliss, and E. Evans. 1999. Analysis of questions asked by family doctors regarding patient care. *BMJ*, 319:358–361.

J. Ely, J. Osheroff, M. Chambliss, M. Ebell, and M. Rosenbaum. 2005. Answering physicians' clinical questions: Obstacles and potential solutions. *Journal of the American Medical Informatics Association*, 12(2):217–224, March-April.

L. Freund, E. Toms, and C. Clarke. 2005. Modeling task-genre relationships for IR in the Workplace. In *Proceedings of SIGIR 2005*.

P. Gorman, J. Ash, and L. Wykoff. 1994. Can primary care physicians' questions be answered using the medical journal literature? *Bulletin of the Medical Library Association*, 82(2):140–146, April.

S. Hauser, D. Demner-Fushman, G. Ford, and G. Thoma. 2004. PubMed on Tap: Discovering design principles for online information delivery to handheld computers. In *Proceedings of MEDINFO 2004*.

R. Haynes, N. Wilczynski, K. McKibbon, C. Walker, and J. Sinclair. 1994. Developing optimal search strategies for detecting clinically sound studies in MEDLINE. *Journal of the American Medical Informatics Association*, 1(6):447–458.

L. Hirschman and R. Gaizauskas. 2001. Natural language question answering: The view from here. *Natural Language Engineering*, 7(4):275–300.

D. Lindberg, B. Humphreys, and A. McCray. 1993. The Unified Medical Language System. *Methods of Information in Medicine*, 32(4):281–291, August.

K. McKeown, N. Elhadad, and V. Hatzivassiloglou. 2003. Leveraging a common representation for personalized search and summarization in a medical digital library. In *Proceedings JCDL 2003*.

E. Mendonça and J. Cimino. 2001. Building a knowledge base to support a digital library. In *Proceedings of MEDINFO 2001*.

D. Moldovan, M. Paşca, S. Harabagiu, and M. Surdeanu. 2002. Performance issues and error analysis in an open-domain question answering system. In *Proceedings of ACL 2002*.

S. Narayanan and S. Harabagiu. 2004. Question answering based on semantic structures. In *Proceedings of COLING 2004*.

Y. Niu and G. Hirst. 2004. Analysis of semantic classes in medical text for question answering. In *Proceedings of the ACL 2004 Workshop on Question Answering in Restricted Domains*.

W. Richardson, M. Wilson, J. Nishikawa, and R. Hayward. 1995. The well-built clinical question: A key to evidence-based decisions. *American College of Physicians Journal Club*, 123(3):A12–A13, November-December.

# Using Scenario Knowledge in Automatic Question Answering

**Sanda Harabagiu and Andrew Hickl**
Language Computer Corporation
1701 North Collins Boulevard
Richardson, Texas 75080 USA
sanda@languagecomputer.com

## Abstract

This paper describes a novel framework for using scenario knowledge in open-domain Question Answering (Q/A) applications that uses a state-of-the-art textual entailment system (Hickl et al., 2006b) in order to discover textual information relevant to the set of topics associated with a scenario description. An intrinsic and an extrinsic evaluation of this method is presented in the context of an automatic Q/A system and results from several user scenarios are discussed.

## 1 Introduction

Users of today's automatic question-answering (Q/A) systems generally have complex information needs that cannot be satisfied by asking single questions in isolation. When users interact with Q/A systems, they often formulate sets of queries that they believe will help them gather the information that needed to perform one or more specific tasks. While human users are generally able to identify their information needs independently, the information needs of organizations are often presented in the form of short prose descriptions – known as *scenarios* – which outline the range of knowledge sought by a customer in order to achieve a specific outcome or to accomplish a particular task. (An example of one scenario is presented in Figure 1.)

Recent work in Q/A has sought to use information derived from these kinds of scenarios in order to retrieve sets of answers that are more relevant – and responsive – to a customer's information needs. While (Harabagiu et al., 2005) used *topic signatures* (Lin and Hovy, 2000; Harabagiu, 2004) computed automatically from collections of documents relevant to a scenario in order to approximate the semantic content of a scenario, (Narayanan and Harabagiu, 2004) employed formal models of the interrelated events, actions, states, and relations implicit to a scenario in order to produce fine-grained, context-sensitive inferences that could be used to answer questions. Scenario knowledge was also included in the form of axiomatic logic transformation developed in (Moldovan et al., 2003). Under this approach, information extracted from the scenario narrative is converted to logical axioms that can used in conjunction with a logic prover in order justify answers returned for questions.

| Scenario Description |
|---|
| The customer has commissioned a research project looking at the impact of the outsourcing of American jobs on the United States' relationship with India. After conducting research on U.S. companies currently doing business in India, the customer wants to know why American corporations have sought to outsource jobs to India, the types of economic advantages that American companies could gain from relocating to India, and the kinds of economic or political inducements that India has offered to American companies looking to outsource jobs there. The customer is not interested in demographic information on Indian employees of American firms. |

Table 1: Example of a User Scenario.

In this paper, we propose that scenario-relevant passages in natural language texts can be identified by recognizing a semantic relation, known as *contextual entailment* (CE), that exists between a text passage and one of a set of subquestions that are conventionally implied by a scenario. Under this model, we expect that a scenario $S$ can be considered to contextually entail a passage $t$, when there exists at least one subquestion $q$ derived from $S$ that textually entails the passage $t$. We show that by using a state-of-the-art textual entailment system (Hickl et al., 2006b), we can provide Q/A systems with another mechanism for approximating the inference between questions and relevant answers. We show how each of these cases of con-



*Proceedings of the Workshop on Task-Focused Summarization and Question Answering*, pages 32–39,
Sydney, July 2006. 

textual entailment can be computed and how it can be used in the intrinsic and extrinsic evaluation of a Q/A system.

The remainder of the paper is organized in the following way. Section 2 introduces our notion of contextual entailment and provides a framework for recognizing instances of CE between scenarios and both questions and answers. Section 3 describes the textual entailment system used at the core of our CE system. Sections 4 and 5 describe separate frameworks for intrinsically and extrinsically evaluating the impact of CE on current Q/A systems. Section 6 presents results from our evaluations, and Section 7 summarizes our conclusions

## 2 Recognizing Contextual Entailment

We define *contextual entailment* (CE) as a directional relation that exists between a text passage $t$ and one of a set of implicit subquestions $q$ that can be derived from a user's interpretation of a scenario. Informally, we consider that a scenario $S$ *contextually entails* a passage $t$ when there exists at least one subquestion $q$ implied by $S$ that can be considered to entail $t$.

We expect that the meaning of an information-seeking scenario $S$ can be represented as a question under discussion (QUD) $Q_S$, which denotes a partially-ordered set of subquestions ($q \in Q_S$) that represent the entire set of questions that could potentially be asked in order to gather information relevant to $S$. Taken together, we expect these subquestions to represent the widest possible construal of a user's information need given $S$.

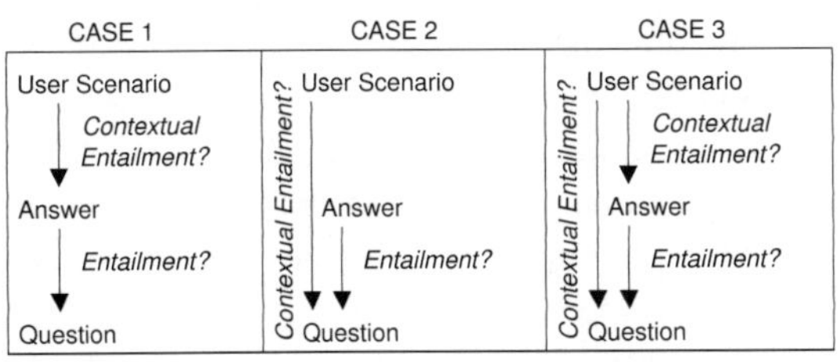


Figure 1: Three types of Contextual Entailment

We believe the set of subquestions implied by $Q_S$ can be used to test whether a text passage is relevant to $S$. Since the formal answerhood relation between a question and its answer(s) can be cast in terms of (logical) entailment (Groenendijk, 1999; Lewis, 1988), we believe that systems for recognizing *textual entailment* (Dagan et al., 2005) could be used in order to identify those text passages that should be considered when gathering information related to a scenario. Based on these assumptions, we expect that the set of text passages that are textually entailed by subquestions derived from a scenario represent information that is more likely to be relevant to the overall topic of the scenario as a whole.

We expect that there are three types of contextual entailment relationships that could prove useful for automatic Q/A systems. First, as illustrated in Case 1 in 1, CE could exist between a scenario and one of the set of answers returned by a Q/A system in response to a user's question. Second, as in Case 2, CE could be established directly between a scenario and the question asked by the user. Finally, as in Case 3, CE could be established both between a scenario and a user's question as well as between a scenario and one of the answers returned by the Q/A system for that question.

Figure 2 provides examples of each of these three types of contextual entailment using the scenario presented in Figure 1.

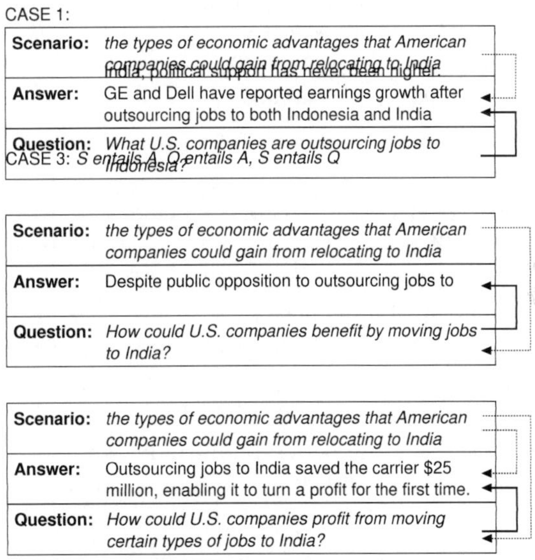


Figure 2: Examples of Contextual Entailment.

In Case 1, the scenario textually entails the meaning of the answer passage, as *earnings growth* from outsourcing necessarily represents one of the types of *economic advantages* that can be derived from outsourcing. However, the scenario cannot be seen as entailing the user's question, as the user's interest in job outsourcing in Indonesia cannot be interpreted as being part of the topics that are associated with the scenario. In this case, recognition of contextual entailment would allow systems to be sensitive to the types of scenario-relevant information that is encountered – even when the user asks questions that are not entailed by the scenario itself. We expect that this type of contextual entailment would allow systems to identify scenario-relevant knowledge throughout a user's interaction with a system, regardless of topic of a user's last query.

In Case 2, the user's question is entailed by the scenario, but no corresponding entailment relationship can be established between the scenario and the answer passage identified by the Q/A system as an answer to the question. While *political support* may be interpretable as one of the benefits realized by companies that outsource, it cannot be understood as one of the *economic advantages* of outsourcing. Here, recognizing that contextual entailment could not be established between the scenario and the answer – but could be established between the scenario and the question – could be used to signal the Q/A system to consider additional answers before moving on to the user's next question. By identifying contextual entailment relationships between answers and elements in a scenario, systems could perform valuable forms of answer validation that could be used to select only the most relevant answers for a user's consideration.

Finally, in Case 3, entailment relationships exist between the scenario and both the user's question and the returned answer, as *saving $25 million* can be considered to be both an *economic advantage* and one of the ways that companies *profit* from outsourcing. In this case, the establishment of contextual entailment could be used to inform topic models that could be used to identify and extract other similarly relevant passages for the user.

In order to capture these three types of CE relationships, we developed the architecture for recognizing contextual entailment illustrated in Figure 3.

This architecture includes three basic types of modules: (1) a *Context Discovery* module, which identifies passages relevant to the concepts mentioned in a scenario, (2) a *Textual Entailment* module, which recognizes implicational relationships between passages, and (3) a *Entailment Merging* module, which ranks relevant passages according to their relevance to the scenario itself. In *Context Discovery*, document retrieval queries are first extracted from each sentence found in a scenario. Once a set of documents has been as-

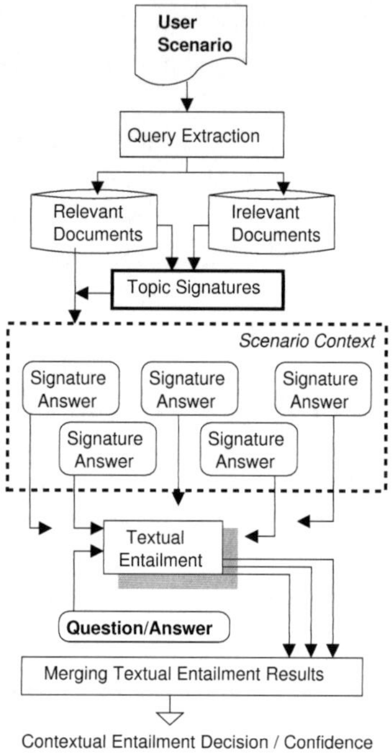

Figure 3: Contextual Entailment Architecture.

sembled, *topic signatures* (Lin and Hovy, 2000; Harabagiu 2004) are computed which identify the set of topic-relevant concepts – and relations between concepts – that are found in the relevant set of documents. Weights associated with each set of topic signatures are then used to extract a set of relevant sentences – referred to as *topic answers* – from each relevant document. Once a set of topic answers have been identified, each topic answer is paired with a question submitted by a user and sent to the *Textual Entailment* system described in Section 2. Topic answers that are deemed to be positive entailments of the user question are assigned a confidence value by the TE system and are then sent to a *Entailment Merging* module, which uses logistic regression in order to rank passages according to their expected relevance to the user scenario. Here, logistic regression is used to find a set of coefficients $b_j$ (where $0 \leq j \leq p$) in order to fit a variable $x$ to a logistic transformation of a probability $q$.

$$\text{logit}(q) = \log \frac{q}{1-q} = b_0 + \sum_{j=1}^{p} b_j x_j + e$$

We believe that since logistic regression uses a maximum likelihood method, it is a suitable technique for normalizing across range of confidence values output by the TE system.

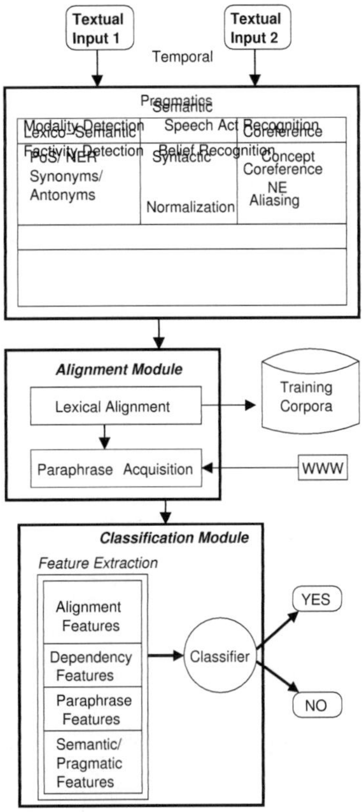


Figure 4: Textual Entailment Architecture.

## 3 Recognizing Textual Entailment

Recent work in computational semantics (Haghighi et al., 2005; Hickl et al., 2006b; MacCartney et al., 2006) has demonstrated the viability of supervised machine learning-based approaches to the recognition of textual entailment (TE). While these approaches have not incorporated the forms of structured world knowledge featured in many logic-based TE systems, classification-based approaches have been consistently among the top-performing systems in both the 2005 and 2006 PASCAL Recognizing Textual Entailment (RTE) Challenges (Dagan et al., 2005), with the best systems (such as (Hickl et al., 2006b)) correctly identifying instances of textual entailment more than 75% of the time.

The architecture of our TE system is presented in Figure 4.[1] Pairs of texts are initially sent to a *Preprocessing Module*, which performs syntactic and semantic parsing of each sentence, resolves coreference, and annotates entities and predicates with a wide range of lexico-semantic and pragmatic information, including named entity information, synonymy and antonymy information, and polarity and modality information.

Once preprocessing is complete, texts are then sent to an *Alignment Module*, which uses *lexical alignment* module in conjunction with a *paraphrase acquisition module* in order to determine the likelihood that pairs of elements selected from each sentence contain corresponding information that could be used in recognizing textual entailment. *Lexical Alignment* is performed using a Maximum Entropy-based classifier which computes an alignment probability $p(a)$ equal to the likelihood that a term selected from one text corresponds to an element selected from another text. Once these pairs of corresponding elements are identified, alignment information is then used in order to extract portions of texts that could be related via one or more phrase-level alternations or "paraphrases". In order to acquire these alternations, the most likely pairs of aligned elements were then sent to a *Paraphrase Acquisition* module, which extracts sentences that contain instances of both aligned elements from the World Wide Web.

Output from these two modules are then combined in a final *Classification Module*, which uses features derived from (1) lexico-semantic properties, (2) semantic dependencies, (3) predicate-based features (including polarity and modality), (4) lexical alignment, and (5) paraphrase acquisition in order learn a decision tree classifier capable of determining whether an entailment relationship exists for a pair of texts.

## 4 Intrinsic Evaluation of Contextual Entailment

Since we believe CE is intrinsic to the Q/A task, we have evaluated the impact of contextual entailment on our Q/A system in two ways. First, we compared the quality of the answers produced, with and without contextual entailment. Second, we evaluated the quality of the ranked list of paragraphs against the list of entailed paragraphs identified by the CE system and the set of relevant answers identified by the Q/A system. This comparison was performed for each of the three cases of entailment presented in Figure 2.

We have explored the impact of knowledge derived from the user scenario through different forms of contextual entailment by comparing the

[1]For more information on the TE system described in this section, please see (Hickl et al., 2006b) and (Harabagiu and Hickl, 2006).

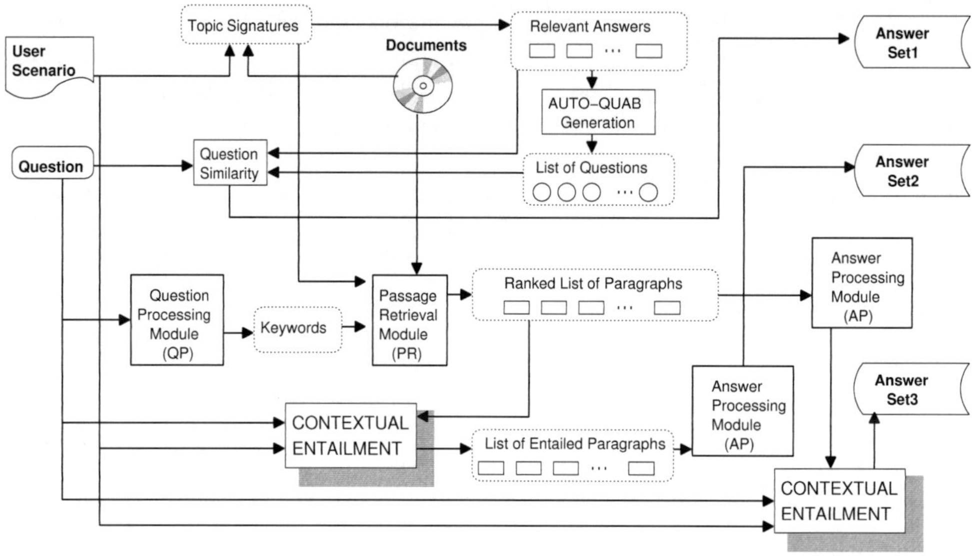


Figure 5: Framework for Intrinsic Evaluation of Contextual Entailment in Q/A.

results of such knowledge integration in a Q/A system against the usage of scenario knowledge reported in (Harabagiu et al., 2005).

Topic signatures, derived from the user scenario and from documents are used to establish text passages that are relevant to the scenario, and thus constitute relevant answers. For each such answer, one or multiple questions were built automatically with the method reported in (Harabagiu et al., 2005). When a new question was asked, its similarity to any of the questions generated based on the knowledge of the scenario is computed, and its corresponding answer is provided as an answer for the current question as well. Since the questions are ranked by similarity to the current question, the answers are also ranked and produce the Answer $Set_1$ illustrated in Figure 5.

When a Q/A system is used for answering the question, the scenario knowledge can be used in two ways. First, the keywords extracted by the Question Processing module can be enhanced with concepts from the topic signatures to produce a ranked list of paragraphs, resulting from the Passage Retrieval Module. These passages together with the question and the user scenario are used in one of the contextual entailment configurations to derive a list of entailed paragraphs from which the Answer Processing module can extract the answer set 2 illustrated in Figure 5. In another way, the ranked list of paragraphs is passed to the Answer Processing module, which provides a set of ranked answers to the contextual entailment configurations to derive a list of entailed answers, represented as answer set 3 in Figure 5. We evaluate the quality of each set of answers, and for the answer set 2 and 3, we produce separate evaluation for each configuration for the contextual entailment.

## 5 Extrinsic Evaluation of Contextual Entailment

Questions asked in response to a user scenario tend to be complex. Following work in (Hickl et al., 2004), we believe complex questions can be answered in one of two ways: either by (1) using techniques (similar to the ones proposed in (Harabagiu et al., 2006)) for automatically decomposing complex questions into sets of informationally-simpler questions, or by (2) using a multi-document summarization (MDS) system (such as the one described in (Lacatusu et al., 2006)) in order to assemble a ranked list of passages which contain information that is potentially relevant to the user's question.

First, we expect that contextual entailment can be used to select the decompositions of a complex question that are most closely related to a scenario. By assigning more confidence to the decompositions that are contextually entailed by a scenario, systems can select a set of answers that are relevant to both the user scenario – and the user's question. In contrast, contextual entailment can be used in conjunction with the output of a MDS system: once a summary has been constructed from the passages retrieved for a query, contextual en-

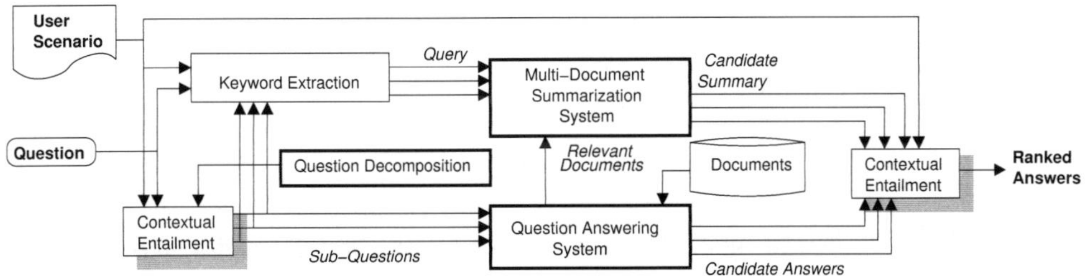


Figure 6: Framework for Extrinsic Evaluation of Contextual Entailment in Q/A.

tailment can be used to select the most relevant sentences from the summary.

The architecture of this proposed system is illustrated in Figure 6.

When using contextual entailment for selecting question decompositions, we rely on the method reported in (Harabagiu et al., 2006) which generates questions by using a random walk on a bipartite graph of salient relations and answers. In this case, the recognition of entailment between questions operates as a filter, forcing questions that are not entailed by any of the signature answers derived from the scenario context (see Figure 3) to be dropped from consideration.

When entailment information is used for reranking candidate answers, the summary is added to the scenario context, each summary sentence being treated akin to a signature answer. We believe that the summary contains the most informative information from both the question and the scenario, since the queries that produced it originated both in the question and in the scenario. By adding summary sentences to the scenario context, we have introduced a new dimension to the processing of the scenario. The contextual entailment is based on the textual entailments between any of the texts from the scenario context and any of the candidate answers.

## 6 Experimental Results

In this section, we present preliminary results from four sets of experiments which show how forms of textual – and contextual – entailment can enhance the quality of answers returned by an automatic Q/A system.

Questions used in these experiments were gathered from human interactions with the interactive Q/A system described in (Hickl et al., 2006a). A total of 6 users were asked to spend approximately 90 minutes gathering information related to three different information-gathering scenarios similar to the one in Table 1. Each user researched two different scenarios, resulting in a total of 12 total research sessions. Once all research sessions were completed, linguistically well-formed questions were extracted from the system logs for each session for use in our experiments; ungrammatical questions or keyword-style queries were not used in our experiments. Table 2 presents a breakdown of the total number of questions collected for each of the 6 scenarios.

| Scenario Name | Users | Total Qs | Avg. Q/Session | $\sigma^2$ |
|---|---|---|---|---|
| $S_1$. India Outsourcing | 4 | 45 | 11.25 | 2.50 |
| $S_2$. Chinese WMD Proliferation | 4 | 38 | 9.50 | 6.45 |
| $S_3$. Libyan Bioweapons Programs | 4 | 63 | 15.75 | 2.22 |
| **Total** | 12 | 146 | 12.17 | 1.23 |

Table 2: Questions Collected from User Experiments.

In order to evaluate the performance of our Q/A system under each of the experimental conditions described below, questions were re-submitted to the Q/A system and the top 10 answers were retrieved. Two annotators were then tasked with judging the correctness – or "relevance" – of each returned answer to the original question. If the answer could be considered to provide either a complete or partial answer to the original question, it was marked as *correct*; if the answer contained information that could not be construed as an answer to the original question, it was marked as *incorrect*.

### 6.1 Textual Entailment

Following (Harabagiu and Hickl, 2006), we used TE information in order to filter answers identified by the Q/A system that were not entailed by the user's original question. After filtering, the top-ranked entailed answer (as determined by the Q/A system) was returned as the system's answer to the question. Results from both a baseline version and a TE-enhanced version of our Q/A system are presented in Table 4.

Although no information from the scenario was used in this experiment, performance of the Q/A

| | | $S_1$ | $S_2$ | $S_3$ | Total |
|---|---|---|---|---|---|
| # of Questions | | 45 | 38 | 63 | 146 |
| baseline | top 1 | 8 (17.78%) | 6 (15.79%) | 11 (17.46%) | 25 (17.12%) |
| TE | top 1 | 10 (22.22%) | 8 (21.05%) | 16 (25.40%) | 34 (23.29%) |
| baseline | top 5 | 17 (37.78%) | 16 (42.11%) | 27 (42.86%) | 60 (41.10%) |
| TE | top 5 | 20 (44.44%) | 17 (44.74%) | 32 (50.79%) | 69 (47.26%) |

Table 3: Impact of Textual Entailment on Q/A.

system increased by more than 6% over the baseline system for each of the three scenarios. These results suggest that TE can be used effectively in order to boost the percentage of relevant answers found in the top answers returned by a system: by focusing only on answers that are entailed by a user's question, we feel that systems can better identify passages that might contain information relevant to a user's information need.

### 6.2 Contextual Entailment

In order to evaluate the performance of our contextual entailment system directly, two annotators were tasked with identifying instances of CE amongst the passages and answers returned by our Q/A system. Annotators were instructed to mark a passage as being *contextually entailed* by a scenario only when the passage could be reasonably expected to be associated with one of the subtopics they believed to be entailed by the complex scenario. If the passage could not be associated with the extension of any subtopic they believed to be entailed by the scenario, annotators were instructed to mark the passage as not being contextually entailed by the scenario. For evaluation purposes, only examples that were marked by both annotators were considered as valid examples of CE.

Annotators were tasked with evaluating three types of output from our Q/A system: (1) the ranked list of passages retrieved by our system's *Passage Retrieval* module, (2) the list of passages identified as being CE by the scenario, and (3) the set of answers marked as being CE by the scenario ($AnsSet_3$). Results from the annotation of these passages are presented in Table 4.

| | $S_1$ | | $S_2$ | | $S_3$ | | Total | |
|---|---|---|---|---|---|---|---|---|
| | # | %Rel | # | %Rel | # | %Rel | # | %Rel |
| Ranked Paragraphs | 450 | 40.4% | 380 | 31.3% | 630 | 42.5% | 1460 | 39.3% |
| Entailed Paragraphs | 112 | 46.5% | 87 | 44.8% | 149 | 52.4% | 348 | 48.6% |
| Answer Set 3 | 304 | 44.4% | 188 | 39.9% | 322 | 49.1% | 814 | 45.2% |

Table 4: Distribution of CE.

Annotators marked 39.3% of retrieved passages as being CE by one of the three scenarios. This number increased substantially when only passages identified by the CE system were considered, as annotators judged 48.6% of CE passages and 45.2% of CE-filtered answers to be valid instances of contextual entailment.

### 6.3 Intrinsic Evaluation

In order to evaluate the impact of CE on a Q/A system, we compared the quality of answers produced (1) when no CE information was used ($AnsSet_1$), (2) when CE information was used to select a list of entailed paragraphs that were submitted to an *Answer Processing* module ($AnsSet_2$), and (3) when CE information was used directly to select answers ($AnsSet_3$). Results from these three experiments are presented in Table 5.

| | | $S_1$ | $S_2$ | $S_3$ | Total |
|---|---|---|---|---|---|
| # of Questions | | 45 | 38 | 63 | 146 |
| $AnsSet_1$ | top 1 | 12 (26.67%) | 9 (23.68%) | 19 (30.16%) | 40 (27.39%) |
| $AnsSet_2$ | top 1 | 16 (35.56%) | 11 (28.95%) | 26 (41.27%) | 53 (36.30%) |
| $AnsSet_3$ | top 1 | 14 (31.11%) | 15 (39.47%) | 31 (49.21%) | 60 (41.09%) |
| $AnsSet_1$ | top 5 | 21 (46.67%) | 17 (44.74%) | 30 (47.62%) | 68 (46.58%) |
| $AnsSet_2$ | top 5 | 24 (53.33%) | 18 (47.37%) | 35 (55.55%) | 77 (52.74%) |
| $AnsSet_3$ | top 5 | 29 (64.44%) | 20 (52.63%) | 39 (61.90%) | 88 (60.27%) |

Table 5: Intrinsic Evaluation of CE on Q/A Performance.

As with the TE-based experiments described in Section 7.1, we found that the Q/A system was more likely to return at least one relevant answer among the top-ranked answers when contextual entailment information was used to either rank or select answers. When CE was used to rank passages for Answer Processing ($AnsSet_2$), accuracy increased by nearly 9% over the baseline ($AnsSet_1$), while accuracy increased by almost 14% overall when CE was used to select answers directly ($AnsSet_3$).

### 6.4 Extrinsic Evaluation

In order to evaluate the performance of the framework illustrated in Figure 6, we compared the performance of a question-focused MDS system (first described in (Lacatusu et al., 2006)) that did not use CE with a similar system that used CE to rank passages for a summary answer.

When CE was not used, sentences identified by the system's Q/A and MDS system for each question were combined and ranked based on number of question keywords found in each sentence. In the CE-enabled system (analogous to the system depicted in Figure 6), only the sentences that were contextually entailed by the scenario were considered; sentences were then ranked using the real-valued *entailment confidence* computed by the CE system for each sentence. Results from this system are presented in Table 6.

Although the CE-enabled system was more likely to return a scenario-relevant sentence in top

| | | $S_1$ | $S_2$ | $S_3$ | Total |
|---|---|---|---|---|---|
| # of Questions | | 45 | 38 | 63 | 146 |
| Without CE | top 1 | 14 (31.11%) | 15 (39.47%) | 31 (49.21%) | 60 (41.09%) |
| With CE | top 1 | 20 (44.44%) | 16 (42.11%) | 32 (50.79%) | 68 (48.23%) |
| Without CE | top 5 | 29 (64.44%) | 20 (52.63%) | 39 (61.90%) | 88 (60.27%) |
| With CE | top 5 | 29 (64.44%) | 21 (55.26%) | 40 (63.49%) | 90 (61.64%) |

Table 6: Extrinsic Evaluation.

position (48.23%) than the system that did not use CE (41.09%), differences between the systems were much less apparent when the top 5 answers returned by each system were compared.

## 7 Conclusions

This paper introduced a new form of textual entailment, known as contextual entailment, which can be used to recognize scenario-relevant information in both the questions users ask and in the answers that automatic Q/A systems return. In addition to outlining a framework for recognizing contextual entailment in texts, we showed that contextual entailment information can significantly enhance the quality of answers returned by a Q/A system in response to users' questions about a particular scenario. In our evaluations, we found that using contextual entailment allowed Q/A systems to improve their accuracy by more than 10% overall.

## 8 Acknowledgments

This material is based upon work funded in whole or in part by the U.S. Government and any opinions, findings, conclusions, or recommendations expressed in this material are those of the authors and do not necessarily reflect the views of the U.S. Government.

## References

Ido Dagan, Oren Glickman, and Bernardo Magnini. 2005. The PASCAL Recognizing Textual Entailment Challenge. In *Proceedings of the PASCAL Challenges Workshop*.

Jeroen Groenendijk. 1999. The logic of interrogation: Classical version. In *Proceedings of the Ninth Semantics and Linguistics Theory Conference (SALT IX)*, Ithaca, NY.

Aria Haghighi, Andrew Ng, and Christopher Manning. 2005. Robust textual inference via graph matching. In *Proceedings of Human Language Technology Conference and Conference on Empirical Methods in Natural Language Processing*, Vancouver, British Columbia, Canada, October.

Sanda Harabagiu and Andrew Hickl. 2006. Methods for using textual entailment in open-domain question-answering. In *Proceedings of the Joint International Conference on Computational Linguistics and Annual Meeting of the Association for Computational Linguistics (COLING-ACL 2006)*, Sydney, Australia.

Sanda Harabagiu, Andrew Hickl, John Lehmann, and Dan Moldovan. 2005. Experiments with Interactive Question-Answering. In *Proceedings of the 43rd Annual Meeting of the Association for Computational Linguistics (ACL'05)*.

Sanda Harabagiu, Finley Lacatusu, and Andrew Hickl. 2006. Answering complex questions with random walk models. In *2006 ACM SIGIR Conference on Research and Development in Information Retrieval (SIGIR)*, Seattle, WA.

Sanda Harabagiu. 2004. Incremental Topic Representations. In *Proceedings of the 20th COLING Conference*, Geneva, Switzerland.

Andrew Hickl, John Lehmann, John Williams, and Sanda Harabagiu. 2004. Experiments with Interactive Question-Answering in Complex Scenarios. In *Proceedings of the Workshop on the Pragmatics of Question Answering at HLT-NAACL 2004*, Boston, MA.

Andrew Hickl, Patrick Wang, John Lehmann, and Sanda Harabagiu. 2006a. FERRET: Interactive Question-Answering for Real-World Environments. In *Proceedings of the Joint International Conference on Computational Linguistics and Annual Meeting of the Association for Computational Linguistics (COLING-ACL 2006) Interactive Presentations Program*, Sydney, Australia.

Andrew Hickl, John Williams, Jeremy Bensley, Kirk Roberts, Bryan Rink, and Ying Shi. 2006b. Recognizing Textual Entailment with LCC's Groundhog System. In *Proceedings of the Second PASCAL Challenges Workshop*, Sydney, Australia.

Finley Lacatusu, Andrew Hickl, Kirk Roberts, Ying Shi, Jeremy Bensley, Bryan Rink, Patrick Wang, and Lara Taylor. 2006. LCC's GISTexter at DUC 2006: Multi-Strategy Multi-Document Summarization. In *Proceedings of the 2006 Document Understanding Conference (DUC 2006)*, New York, New York.

David Lewis. 1988. Relevant Implication. *Theoria*, 54(3):161–174.

Chin-Yew Lin and Eduard Hovy. 2000. The automated acquisition of topic signatures for text summarization. In *Proceedings of the 18th COLING Conference*, Saarbrücken, Germany.

Bill MacCartney, Trond Grenager, Marie-Catherine de Marneffe, Daniel Cer, and Christopher D. Manning. 2006. Learning to recognize features of valid textual entailments. In *Proceedings of the Joint Human Language Technology Conference and Annual Meeting of the North American Chapter of the Association for Computational Linguistics (HLT-NAACL 2006)*, New York, New York.

Dan Moldovan, Christine Clark, Sanda Harabagiu, and Steve Maiorano. 2003. COGEX: A Logic Prover for Question Answering. In *Proceedings of HLT/NAACL-2003*.

Srini Narayanan and Sanda Harabagiu. 2004. Question Answering based on Semantic Structures. In *Proceedings of COLING-2004*.

# Automating Help-desk Responses: A Comparative Study of Information-gathering Approaches

**Yuval Marom and Ingrid Zukerman**
Faculty of Information Technology
Monash University
Clayton, VICTORIA 3800, AUSTRALIA
{yuvalm,ingrid}@csse.monash.edu.au

## Abstract

We present a comparative study of corpus-based methods for the automatic synthesis of email responses to help-desk requests. Our methods were developed by considering two operational dimensions: (1) information-gathering technique, and (2) granularity of the information. In particular, we investigate two techniques – retrieval and prediction – applied to information represented at two levels of granularity – sentence-level and document level. We also developed a hybrid method that combines prediction with retrieval. Our results show that the different approaches are applicable in different situations, addressing a combined 72% of the requests with either complete or partial responses.

## 1 Introduction

Email inquiries sent to help desks often "revolve around a small set of common questions and issues".[1] This means that help-desk operators spend most of their time dealing with problems that have been previously addressed. Further, a significant proportion of help-desk responses contain a low level of technical content, corresponding, for example, to inquires addressed to the wrong group, or insufficient detail provided by the customer about his or her problem. Organizations and clients would benefit if the efforts of human operators were focused on difficult, atypical problems, and an automated process was employed to deal with the easier problems.

In this paper, we report on our experiments with corpus-based approaches to the automation of help-desk responses. Our study is based on a corpus of 30,000 email dialogues between users and help-desk operators at Hewlett-Packard. These dialogues deal with a variety of user requests, which include requests for technical assistance, inquiries about products, and queries about how to return faulty products or parts.

In order to restrict the scope of our study, we considered two-turn short dialogues, comprising a request followed by an answer, where the answer has at most 15 lines. This yields a sub-corpus of 6659 dialogues. As a first step, we have automatically clustered the corpus according to the subject line of the first email. This process yielded 15 topic-based datasets that contain between 135 and 1200 email dialogues. Owing to time limitations, the procedures described in this paper were applied to 8 of the datasets, corresponding to approximately 75% of the dialogues.

Analysis of our corpus yields the following observations.

- **O1:** Requests containing precise information, such as product names or part specifications, sometimes elicit helpful, precise answers referring to this information, while other times they elicit answers that do not refer to the query terms, but contain generic information (e.g., referring customers to another help group or asking them to call a particular phone number). Request-answer pair **RA1** in Figure 1 illustrates the first situation, while the pair **RA2** illustrates the second.[2]

[1] http://customercare.telephonyonline.com/ar/telecom_next_generation_customer.

[2] Our examples are reproduced verbatim from the corpus (except for URLs and phone numbers which have been disguised by us), and some have user or operator errors.



*Proceedings of the Workshop on Task-Focused Summarization and Question Answering*, pages 40–47,
Sydney, July 2006. 

**RA1:**
*Do I need Compaq driver software for my armada 1500 docking station? This in order to be able to re-install win 98?*
I would recommend to install the latest system rompaq, on the laptop and the docking station. Just select the model of computer and the operating system you have. `http://www.thislink.com`.

**RA2:**
*Is there a way to disable the NAT firewall on the Compaq CP-2W so I don't get a private ip address through the wireless network?*
Unfortunately, you have reached the incorrect eResponse queue for your unit. Your device is supported at the following link, or at `888-phone-number`. We apologize for the inconvenience.

Figure 1: Sample request-answer pairs.

**A3:**
If you are able to see the Internet then it sounds like it is working, you may want to get in touch with your IT department to see if you need to make any changes to your settings to get it to work. *Try performing a soft reset, by pressing the stylus pen in the small hole on the bottom left hand side of the Ipaq and then release.*

**A4:**
*I would recommend doing a soft reset by pressing the stylus pen in the small hole on the left hand side of the Ipaq and then release.* Then charge the unit overnight to make sure it has been long enough and then see what happens. If the battery is not charging then the unit will need to be sent in for repair.

Figure 2: Sample answers that share a sentence.

- **O2:** Operators tend to re-use the same sentences in different responses. This is partly a result of companies having in-house manuals that prescribe how to generate an answer. For instance, answers **A3** and **A4** in Figure 2 share the sentence in italics.

These observations prompt us to consider complementary approaches along two separate dimensions of our problem. The first dimension pertains to the *technique applied to determine the information in an answer*, and the second dimension pertains to the *granularity of the information*.

- Observation **O1** leads us to consider two techniques for obtaining information: *retrieval* and *prediction*. Retrieval returns an information item by matching its terms to query terms (Salton and McGill, 1983). Hence, it is likely to obtain precise information if available. In contrast, prediction uses features of requests and responses to select an information item. For example, the absence of a particular term in a request may be a good predictive feature (which cannot be considered in traditional retrieval). Thus, prediction could yield replies that do not match particular query terms.

- Observation **O2** leads us to consider two levels of granularity: *document* and *sentence*. That is, we can obtain a document comprising a complete answer on the basis of a request (i.e., re-use an answer to a previous request), or we can obtain individual sentences and then combine them to compose an answer, as is done in multi-document summarization (Filatova and Hatzivassiloglou, 2004). The sentence-level granularity enables the re-use of a sentence for different responses, as well as the composition of partial responses.

The methods developed on the basis of these two dimensions are: *Retrieve Answer, Predict Answer, Predict Sentences, Retrieve Sentences* and *Hybrid Predict-Retrieve Sentences*. The first four methods represent the possible combinations of information-gathering technique and level of granularity; the fifth method is a hybrid where the two information-gathering techniques are applied at the sentence level. The generation of responses under these different methods combines different aspects of document retrieval, question-answering, and multi-document summarization.

Our aim in this paper is to investigate when the different methods are applicable, and whether individual methods are uniquely successful in certain situations. For this purpose, we decided to assign a level of success not only to complete responses, but also to partial ones (obtained with the sentence-based methods). The rationale for this is that we believe that a partial high-precision response is better than no response, and better than a complete response that contains incorrect information. We plan to test these assumptions in future user studies.

The rest of this paper is organized as follows. In the next section, we describe our five methods, followed by the evaluation of their results. In Section 4, we discuss related research, and then present our conclusions and plans for future work.

## 2 Information-gathering Methods

### 2.1 Retrieve a Complete Answer

This method retrieves a complete document (answer) on the basis of request lemmas. We use cosine similarity to determine a retrieval score, and use a minimal retrieval threshold that must be surpassed for a response to be accepted.

We have considered three approaches to indexing the answers in our corpus: according to the content lemmas in (1) requests, (2) answers, or (3) requests&answers. The results in Section 3 are for the third approach, which proved best. To illustrate the difference between these approaches, consider request-answer pair **RA2**. If we received a new request similar to that in **RA2**, the answer in **RA2** would be retrieved if we had indexed according to requests or requests&answers. However, if we had indexed only on answers, then the response would not be retrieved.

### 2.2 Predict a Complete Answer

This prediction method first groups similar answers in the corpus into answer clusters. For each request, we then predict an answer cluster on the basis of the request features, and select the answer that is most representative of the cluster (closest to the centroid). This method would predict a group of answers similar to the answer in **RA2** from the input lemmas "compaq" and "cp-2w".

The clustering is performed in advance of the prediction process by the intrinsic classification program *Snob* (Wallace and Boulton, 1968), using the content lemmas (unigrams) in the answers as features. The predictive model is a Decision Graph (Oliver, 1993) trained on (1) input features: unigram and bigram lemmas in the request,[3] and (2) target feature – the identifier of the answer cluster that contains the actual answer for the request.[4] The model provides a prediction of which response cluster is most suitable for a given request, as well as a level of confidence in this prediction. We do not attempt to produce an answer if the confidence is not sufficiently high.

In principle, rather than clustering the answers, the predictive model could have been trained on individual answers. However, on one hand, the dimensionality of this task is very high, and on the other hand, answers that share significant features would be predicted together, effectively acting as a cluster. By clustering answers in advance, we reduce the dimensionality of the problem, at the expense of some loss of information (since somewhat dissimilar answers may be grouped together).

### 2.3 Predict Sentences

This method looks at each answer sentence as though it were a separate document, and groups similar sentences into clusters in order to obtain meaningful sentence abstractions and avoid redundancy.[5] For instance, the last sentence in **A3** and the first sentence in **A4** are assigned to the same sentence cluster. As for Answer Prediction (Section 2.2), this clustering process also reduces the dimensionality of the problem.

Each request is used to predict promising clusters of answer sentences, and an answer is composed by extracting a sentence from such clusters. Because the sentences in each cluster originate in different response documents, the process of selecting them for a new response corresponds to multi-document summarization. In fact, our selection mechanism, described in more detail in (Marom and Zukerman, 2005), is based on a multi-document summarization formulation proposed by Filatova and Hatzivassiloglou (2004).

In order to be able to generate appropriate answers in this manner, the sentence clusters should be *cohesive*, and they should be predicted with high confidence. A cluster is cohesive if the sentences in it are similar to each other. This means that it is possible to obtain a sentence that represents the cluster adequately (which is not the case for an uncohesive cluster). A high-confidence prediction indicates that the sentence is relevant to many requests that share certain regularities. Owing to these requirements, the Sentence Prediction method will often produce partial answers (i.e., it will have a high precision, but often a low recall).

#### 2.3.1 Sentence clustering

The clustering is performed by applying *Snob* using the following sentence-based and word-based features, all of which proved significant for

[3]Significant bigrams are obtained using the NSP package (`http://www.d.umn.edu/~tpederse/nsp.html`).

[4]At present, the clustering features differ from the prediction features because these parts of the system were developed at different times. In the near future, we will align these features.

[5]We did not cluster request sentences, as requests are often ungrammatical, which makes it hard to segment them into sentences, and the language used in requests is more diverse than the corporate language used in responses.

at least some datasets. The sentence-based features are:

- Number of syntactic phrases in the sentence (e.g., prepositional, subordinate) – gives an idea of sentence complexity.
- Grammatical mood of the main clause (5 states: imperative, imperative-step, declarative, declarative-step, unknown) – indicates the function of the sentence in the answer, e.g., an isolated instruction, part of a sequence of steps, part of a list of options.
- Grammatical person in the subject of the main clause (4 states: first, second, third, unknown) – indicates the agent (e.g., organization or client) or patient (e.g., product).

The word-based features are binary:

- Significant lemma bigrams in the subject of the main clause and in the "augmented" object in the main clause. This is the syntactic object if it exists or the subject of a prepositional phrase in an imperative sentence with no object, e.g., "click on *the following link*."
- The verbs in the sentence and their polarity (asserted or negated).
- All unigrams in the sentence, excluding verbs.

#### 2.3.2 Calculation of cluster cohesion

To measure the textual cohesion of a cluster, we inspect the centroid values corresponding to the word features. Due to their binary representation, the centroid values correspond to probabilities of the words appearing in the cluster. Our measure is similar to entropy, in the sense that it yields nonzero values for extreme probabilities (Marom and Zukerman, 2005). It implements that idea that a cohesive group of sentences should agree strongly on both the words that appear in these sentences and the words that are omitted. Hence, it is possible to obtain a sentence that adequately represents a cohesive sentence cluster, while this is not the case for a loose sentence cluster. For example, the italicized sentences in **A3** and **A4** belong to a highly cohesive sentence cluster (0.93), while the opening answer sentence in **RA1** belongs to a less cohesive cluster (0.7) that contains diverse sentences about the Rompaq power management.

#### 2.3.3 Sentence-cluster prediction

Unlike Answer Prediction, we use a Support Vector Machine (SVM) for predicting sentence clusters. A separate SVM is trained for each sentence cluster, with unigram and bigram lemmas in a request as input features, and a binary target feature specifying whether the cluster contains a sentence from the response to this request.

During the prediction stage, the SVMs predict zero or more clusters for each request. One representative sentence (closest to the centroid) is then extracted from each highly cohesive cluster predicted with high confidence. These sentences will appear in the answer (at present, these sentences are treated as a set, and are not organized into a coherent reply).

### 2.4 Retrieve Sentences

As for Sentence Prediction (Section 2.3), this method looks at each answer sentence as though it were a separate document. For each request sentence, we retrieve candidate answer sentences on the basis of the match between the content lemmas in the request sentence and the answer sentence. For example, while the first answer sentence in **RA1** might match the first request sentence in **RA1**, an answer sentence from a different response (about re-installing Win98) might match the second request sentence. The selection of individual text units from documents implements ideas from question-answering approaches.

We are mainly interested in answer sentences that "cover" request sentences, i.e., the terms in the request should appear in the answer. Hence, we use *recall* as the measure for the goodness of a match, where recall is defined as follows.

$$recall = \frac{\text{TF.IDF of lemmas in request sent \& answer sent}}{\text{TF.IDF of lemmas in request sentence}}$$

We initially retain the answer sentences whose recall exceeds a threshold.[6]

Once we have the set of candidate answer sentences, we attempt to remove redundant sentences. This requires the identification of sentences that are similar to each other — a task for which we use the sentence clusters described in Section 2.3. Again, this redundancy-removal step essentially casts the task as multi-document summarization. Given a group of answer sentences that belong to

[6]To assess the goodness of a sentence, we experimented with *f-scores* that had different weights for recall and precision. Our results were insensitive to these variations.

the same cohesive cluster, we retain the sentence with the highest recall (in our current trials, a cluster is sufficiently cohesive for this purpose if its cohesion $\geq 0.7$). In addition, we retain all the answer sentences that do not belong to a cohesive cluster. All the retained sentences will appear in the answer.

### 2.5 Hybrid Predict-Retrieve Sentences

It is possible that the Sentence Prediction method predicts a sentence cluster that is not sufficiently cohesive for a confident selection of a representative sentence, but instead the ambiguity can be resolved through cues in the request. For example, selecting between a group of sentences concerning the installation of different drivers might be possible if the request mentions a specific driver. Thus the Sentence Prediction method is complemented with the Sentence Retrieval method to form a hybrid, as follows.

- For highly cohesive clusters predicted with high confidence, we select a representative sentence as before.
- For clusters with medium cohesion predicted with high confidence, we attempt to match the sentences with the request sentences, using the Sentence Retrieval method but with a lower recall threshold. This reduction takes place because the high prediction confidence provides a guarantee that the sentences in the cluster are suitable for the request, so there is no need for a convervative recall threshold. The role of retrieval is now to select the sentence whose content lemmas best match the request.
- For uncohesive clusters or clusters predicted with low confidence, we have to resort to word matches, which means reverting to the higher, more convervative recall threshold, because we no longer have the prediction confidence.

## 3 Evaluation

As mentioned in Section 1, our corpus was divided into topic-based datasets. We have observed that the different datasets lend themselves differently to the various information-gathering methods described in the previous section. In this section, we examine the overall performance of the five methods across the corpus, as well as their performance for different datasets.

### 3.1 Measures

We are interested in two performance indicators: *coverage* and *quality*.

**Coverage** is the proportion of requests for which a response can be generated. The various information gathering methods presented in the previous section have acceptance criteria that indicate that there is some level of confidence in generating a response. A request for which a planned response fails to meet these criteria is not covered, or addressed, by the system. We are interested in seeing if the different methods are applicable in different situations, that is, how exclusively they address different requests. Note that the sentence-based methods generate partial responses, which are considered acceptable so long as they contain at least one sentence generated with high confidence. In many cases these methods produce obvious and non-informative sentences such as "Thank you for contacting HP", which would be deemed an acceptable response. We have manually excluded such sentences from the calculation of coverage, in order to have a more informative comparison between the different methods.

Ideally, the **quality** of the generated responses should be measured through a user study, where people judge the correctness and appropriateness of answers generated by the different methods. However, we intend to refine our methods further before we conduct such a study. Hence, at present we rely on a text-based quantitative measure. Our experimental setup involves a standard 10-fold validation procedure, where we repeatedly train on 90% of a dataset and test on the remaining 10%. We then evaluate the quality of the answers generated for the requests in each test split, by comparing them with the actual responses given by the help-desk operator for these requests.

We are interested in two quality measures: (1) the precision of a generated response, and (2) its overall similarity to the actual response. The reason for this distinction is that the former does not penalize for a low recall — it simply measures how correct the generated text is. As stated in Section 1, a partial but correct response may be better than a complete response that contains incorrect units of information. On the other hand, more complete responses are favoured over partial ones, and so we use the second measure to get an overall indication of how correct and complete a response is. We use the traditional Information

Table 1: Performance of the different methods, measured as coverage, precision and f-score.

| Method | Coverage | Precision Ave (stdev) | F-score Ave (stdev) |
|---|---|---|---|
| Answer Retrieval | 43% | 0.37 (0.34) | 0.35 (0.33) |
| Answer Prediction | 29% | 0.82 (0.21) | 0.82 (0.24) |
| Sentence Prediction | 34% | 0.94 (0.13) | 0.78 (0.18) |
| Sentence Retrieval | 9% | 0.19 (0.19) | 0.12 (0.11) |
| Sentence Hybrid | 43% | 0.81 (0.29) | 0.66 (0.25) |
| Combined | 72% | 0.80 (0.25) | 0.50 (0.33) |

Retrieval precision and f-score measures (Salton and McGill, 1983), employed on a word-by-word basis, to evaluate the quality of the generated responses.[7]

### 3.2 Results

Table 1 shows the overall results obtained using the different methods. We see that combined the different methods can address 72% of the requests. That is, at least one of these methods can produce some non-empty response to 72% of the requests. Looking at the individual coverages of the different methods we see that they must be applicable in different situations, because the highest individual coverage is 43%.

The Answer Retrieval method addresses 43% of the requests, and in fact, about half of these (22%) are uniquely addressed by this method. However, in terms of the quality of the generated response, we see that the performance is very poor (both precision and f-score have very low averages). Nevertheless, there are some cases where this method uniquely addresses requests quite well. In three of the datasets, Answer Retrieval is the only method that produces good answers, successfully addressing 15-20 requests (about 5% of the requests in these datasets). These requests include several cases similar to **RA2**, where the request was sent to the wrong place. We would expect Answer Prediction to be able to handle such cases as well. However, when there are not enough similar cases in the dataset (as is the case with the three datasets referred to above), Answer Prediction is not able to generalize from them, and therefore we can only rely on a new request closely matching an old request or an old answer.

The Answer Prediction method can address 29% of the requests. Only about a tenth of these are uniquely addressed by this method, but the generated responses are of a fairly high quality, with an average precision and f-score of 0.82. Notice the large standard deviation of these averages, suggesting a somewhat inconsistent behaviour. This is due to the fact that this method gives good results only when complete template responses are found. In this case, any re-used response will have a high similarity to the actual response. However, when this is not the case, the performance degrades substantially, resulting in inconsistent behaviour. This behaviour is particularly prevalent for the "product replacement" dataset, which comprises 18% of the requests. The vast majority of the requests in this dataset ask for a return shipping label to be mailed to the customer, so that he or she can return a faulty product. Although these requests often contain detailed product descriptions, the responses rarely refer to the actual products, and often contain the following generic answer.

**A5:**
Your request for a return airbill has been received and has been sent for processing. Your replacement airbill will be sent to you via email within 24 hours.

Answer Retrieval fails in such cases, because each request has precise information about the actual product, so a new request can neither match an old request (about a different product) nor can it match the generic response. In contrast, Answer Prediction can ignore the precise information in the request, and infer from the mention of a shipping label that the generic response is appropriate. When we exclude this dataset from the calculations, both the average precision and f-score for the Answer Prediction method fall below those of the Sentence Prediction and Hybrid methods. This means that Answer Prediction is suitable when requests that share some regularity receive a complete template answer.

The Sentence Prediction method can find reg-

[7] We have also employed sequence-based measures using the ROUGE tool set (Lin and Hovy, 2003), with similar results to those obtained with the word-by-word measure.

ularities at the sub-document level, and therefore deal with cases when partial responses can be generated. It produces such responses for 34% of the requests, and does so with a consistently high precision (average 0.94, standard deviation 0.13). Only an overall 1% of the requests are uniquely addressed by this method, however, for the cases that are shared between this method and other ones, it is useful to compare the actual quality of the generated response. In 5% of the cases, the Sentence Prediction method either uniquely addresses requests, or jointly addresses requests together with other methods but has a higher f-score. This means that in some cases a partial response has a higher quality than a complete one.

Like the document-level Answer Retrieval method, the Sentence Retrieval method performs poorly. It is difficult to find an answer sentence that closely matches a request sentence, and even when this is possible, the selected sentences tend to be different to the ones used by the help-desk operators, hence the low precision and f-score. This is discussed further below in the context of the Sentence Hybrid method.

The Sentence Hybrid method extends the Sentence Prediction method by employing sentence retrieval as well, and thus has a higher coverage (45%). In fact, the retrieval component serves to disambiguate between groups of candidate sentences, thus enabling more sentences to be included in the generated response. This, however, is at the expense of precision, as we also saw for the pure Sentence Retrieval method. Although retrieval selects sentences that match closely a given request, this selection can differ from the "selections" made by the operator in the actual response. Precision (and hence f-score) penalizes such sentences, even when they are more appropriate than those in the model response. For example, consider request-answer pair **RA6**. The answer is quite generic, and is used almost identically for several other requests. The Hybrid method almost reproduces this answer, replacing the first sentence with **A7**. This sentence, which matches more request words than the first sentence in the model answer, was selected from a sentence cluster that is not highly cohesive, and contains sentences that describe different reasons for setting up a repair (the matching word in **A7** is "screen"). The Hybrid method outperforms the other methods in about 10% of the cases, where it either

**RA6:**
*My screen is coming up reversed (mirrored). There must be something loose electronically because if I put the stylus in it's hole and move it back and forth, I can get the screen to display properly momentarily. Please advise where to send for repairs.*
To get the iPAQ serviced, you can call `1-800-phone-number`, options 3, 1 (enter a 10 digit phone number), 2. Enter your phone number twice and then wait for the routing center to put you through to a technician with Technical Support. They can get the unit picked up and brought to our service center.

**A7:**
To get the iPAQ repaired (battery, stylus lock and screen), please call `1-800-phone-number`, options 3, 1 (enter a 10 digit phone number), 2.

uniquely addresses requests, or addresses them jointly with other methods but produces responses with a higher f-score.

### 3.3 Summary

In summary, our results show that each of the different methods is applicable in different situations, all occurring significantly in the corpus, with the exception of the Sentence Retrieval method. The Answer Retrieval method uniquely addresses a large portion of the requests, but many of its attempts are spurious, thus lowering the combined overall quality shown at the bottom of Table 1 (average f-score 0.50), calculated by using the best performing method for each request. The Answer Prediction method is good at addressing situations that warrant complete template responses. However, its confidence criteria might need refining to lower the variability in quality. The combined contribution of the sentence-based methods is substantial (about 15%), suggesting that partial responses of high precision may be better than complete responses with a lower precision.

## 4 Related Research

There are very few reported attempts at corpus-based automation of help-desk responses. The retrieval system *eResponder* (Carmel et al., 2000) is similar to our Answer Retrieval method, where the system retrieves a list of request-response pairs and presents a ranked list of responses to the user. Our results show that due to the repetitions in the responses, multi-document summarization can be used to produce a single (possibly partial) representative response. This is recognized by Berger and Mittal (2000), who employ query-relevant summarization to generate responses. However, their corpus consists of FAQ request-response pairs — a significantly different corpus to ours in that it lacks repetition and redundancy, and where the responses are not personalized. Lapalme and Kosseim (2003) propose a retrieval approach similar to our Answer Retrieval method, and a question-answering approach, but applied to a corpus of technical documents rather than request-response pairs. The methods presented in this paper combine different aspects of document retrieval, question-answering and multi-document summarization, applied to a corpus of repetitive request-response pairs.

## 5 Conclusion and Future Work

We have presented four basic methods and one hybrid method for addressing help-desk requests. The basic methods represent the four ways of combining level of granularity (sentence and document) with information-gathering technique (prediction and retrieval). The hybrid method applies prediction possibly followed by retrieval to information at the sentence level. The results show that with the exception of Sentence Retrieval, the different methods can address a significant portion of the requests. A future avenue of research is thus to characterize situations where different methods are applicable, in order to derive decision procedures that determine the best method automatically. We have also started to investigate an intermediate level of granularity: paragraphs.

Our results suggest that the automatic evaluation method requires further consideration. As seen in Section 3, our f-score penalizes the Sentence Prediction and Hybrid methods when they produce good answers that are more informative than the model answer. As mentioned previously, a user study would provide a more conclusive evaluation of the system, and could be used to determine preferences regarding partial responses.

Finally, we propose the following extensions to our current implementation. First, we would like to improve the representation used for clustering, prediction and retrieval by using features that incorporate word-based similarity metrics (Pedersen et al., 2004). Secondly, we intend to investigate a more focused sentence retrieval approach that utilizes syntactic matching of sentences. For example, if a sentence cluster is strongly predicted by a request, but the cluster is uncohesive because of a low verb agreement, then the retrieval should favour the sentences whose verbs match those in the request.


## Acknowledgments

This research was supported in part by grant LP0347470 from the Australian Research Council and by an endowment from Hewlett-Packard. The authors also thank Hewlett-Packard for the extensive help-desk data, and Tony Tony for assistance with the sentence-segmentation software, and Kerri Morgan and Michael Niemann for developing the syntactic feature extraction code.


## References


A. Berger and V.O. Mittal. 2000. Query-relevant summarization using FAQs. In *ACL2000 – Proceedings of the 38th Annual Meeting of the Association for Computational Linguistics*, pages 294–301, Hong Kong.

D. Carmel, M. Shtalhaim, and A. Soffer. 2000. eResponder: Electronic question responder. In *CoopIS '02: Proceedings of the 7th International Conference on Cooperative Information Systems*, pages 150–161, Eilat, Israel.

E. Filatova and V. Hatzivassiloglou. 2004. A formal model for information selection in multi-sentence text extraction. In *COLING'04 – Proceedings of the 20th International Conference on Computational Linguistics*, pages 397–403, Geneva, Switzerland.

G. Lapalme and L. Kosseim. 2003. Mercure: Towards an automatic e-mail follow-up system. *IEEE Computational Intelligence Bulletin*, 2(1):14–18.

C.Y. Lin and E.H. Hovy. 2003. Automatic evaluation of summaries using n-gram co-occurrence statistics. In *Proceedings of the 2003 Language Technology Conference (HLT-NAACL 2003)*, Edmonton, Canada.

Y. Marom and I. Zukerman. 2005. Towards a framework for collating help-desk responses from multiple documents. In *Proceedings of the IJCAI05 Workshop on Knowledge and Reasoning for Answering Questions*, pages 32–39, Edinburgh, Scotland.

J.J. Oliver. 1993. Decision graphs – an extension of decision trees. In *Proceedings of the Fourth International Workshop on Artificial Intelligence and Statistics*, pages 343–350, Fort Lauderdale, Florida.

T. Pedersen, S. Patwardhan, and J. Michelizzi. 2004. WordNet::Similarity – measuring the relatedness of concepts. In *AAAI-04 – Proceedings of the Nineteenth National Conference on Artificial Intelligence*, pages 25–29, San Jose, California.

G. Salton and M.J. McGill. 1983. *An Introduction to Modern Information Retrieval*. McGraw Hill.

C.S. Wallace and D.M. Boulton. 1968. An information measure for classification. *The Computer Journal*, 11(2):185–194.

# DUC 2005: Evaluation of Question-Focused Summarization Systems

**Hoa Trang Dang**
Information Access Division
National Institute of Standards and Technology
100 Bureau Drive
Gaithersburg, MD, 20899
hoa.dang@nist.gov

## Abstract

The Document Understanding Conference (DUC) 2005 evaluation had a single user-oriented, question-focused summarization task, which was to synthesize from a set of 25-50 documents a well-organized, fluent answer to a complex question. The evaluation shows that the best summarization systems have difficulty extracting relevant sentences in response to complex questions (as opposed to representative sentences that might be appropriate to a generic summary). The relatively generous allowance of 250 words for each answer also reveals how difficult it is for current summarization systems to produce fluent text from multiple documents.

## 1 Introduction

The Document Understanding Conference (DUC) is a series of evaluations of automatic text summarization systems. It is organized by the National Institute of Standards of Technology with the goals of furthering progress in automatic summarization and enabling researchers to participate in large-scale experiments.

In DUC 2001-2004 a growing number of research groups participated in the evaluation of generic and focused summaries of English newspaper and newswire data. Various target sizes were used (10-400 words) and both single-document summaries and summaries of multiple documents were evaluated (around 10 documents per set). Summaries were manually judged for both content and readability. To evaluate content, each peer (human or automatic) summary was compared against a single model (human) summary using SEE (http://www.isi.edu/ cyl/SEE/) to estimate the percentage of information in the model that was covered in the peer. Additionally, automatic evaluation of content coverage using ROUGE (Lin, 2004) was explored in 2004.

Human summaries vary in both writing style and content. For example, (Harman and Over, 2004) noted that a human summary can vary in its level of *granularity*, whether the summary has a very high-level analysis or primarily contains details. They analyzed the effects of human variaion in the DUC evaluations and concluded that despite large variation in model summaries, the rankings of the systems when compared against a single model for each document set remained stable *when averaged over a large number of document sets* and human assessors. The use of a large test set to smooth over natural human variation is not a new technique; it is the approach that has been taken in TREC (Text Retrieval Conference) for many years (Voorhees and Buckley, 2002).

While evaluators can achieve stable overall system rankings by averaging scores over a large number of document sets, system builders are still faced with the challenge of producing a summary for a given document set that is *most likely* to satisfy any human user (since they cannot know ahead of time which human will be using or judging the summary). Thus, system developers desire an evaluation methodology that takes into account human variation in summaries *for any given document set*.

DUC 2005 marked a major change in direction from previous years. The road mapping committee had strongly recommended that new tasks be undertaken that were strongly tied to a clear user application. At the same time, the program committee wanted to work on new evaluation methodologies and metrics that would take into



*Proceedings of the Workshop on Task-Focused Summarization and Question Answering*, pages 48–55,
Sydney, July 2006. 

account variation of content in human-authored summaries.

Therefore, DUC 2005 had a single user-oriented system task that allowed the community to put some time and effort into helping with a new evaluation framework. The system task modeled real-world complex question answering (Amigo et al., 2004). Systems were to synthesize from a set of 25-50 documents a brief, well-organized, fluent answer to a need for information that could not be met by just stating a name, date, quantity, etc. Summaries were evaluated for both content and readability.

The task design attempted to constrain two parameters that could produce summaries with widely different content: focus and granularity. Having a question to focus the summary was intended to improve agreement in content between the model summaries. Additionally, the assessor who developed each topic specified the desired granularity (level of generalization) of the summary. Granularity was a way to express one type of user preference; one user might want a general background or overview summary, while another user might want specific details that would allow him to answer questions about specific events or situations.

Because it is both impossible and unnatural to eliminate all human variation, our assessors created as many manual summaries as feasible for each topic, to provide examples of the range of normal human variability in the summarization task. These multiple models would provide more representative training data to system developers, while enabling additional experiments to investigate the effect of human variability on the evaluation of summarization systems.

As in past DUCs, assessors manually evaluated each summary for readability using a set of linguistic quality questions. Summary content was manually evaluated using the pseudo-extrinsic measure of responsiveness, which does not attempt pairwise comparison of peers against a model summary but gives a coarse ranking of all the summaries based on responsiveness of the summary to the topic. In parallel, ISI and Columbia University led the summarization research community in two exploratory efforts at intrinsic evaluation of summary content; these evaluations compared peer summaries against multiple reference summaries, using Basic Elements at ISI and Pyramids at Columbia University.

This paper describes the DUC 2005 task and the results of our evaluations of summary content and readability. (Hovy et al., 2005) and (Passonneau et al., 2005) provide additional details and results of the evaluations of summary content using Basic Elements and Pyramids.

## 2 Task Description

The DUC 2005 task was a complex question-focused summarization task that required summarizers to piece together information from multiple documents to answer a question or set of questions as posed in a topic.

Assessors developed a total of 50 topics to be used as test data. For each topic, the assessor selected 25-50 related documents from the *Los Angeles Times* and *Financial Times of London* and formulated a topic statement, which was a request for information that could be answered using the selected documents. The topic statement could be in the form of a question or set of related questions and could include background information that the assessor thought would help clarify his/her information need.

The assessor also indicated the "granularity" of the desired response for each topic. That is, they indicated whether they wanted the answer to their question(s) to name *specific* events, people, places, etc., or whether they wanted a *general*, high-level answer. Only one value of granularity was given for each topic, since the goal was not to measure the effect of different granularities on system performance for a given topic, but to provide additional information about the user's preferences to both human and automatic summarizers.

An example DUC topic follows:

> **num**: D345
> **title**: American Tobacco Companies Overseas
> **narr**: In the early 1990's, American tobacco companies tried to expand their business overseas. What did these companies do or try to do and where? How did their parent companies fare?
> **granularity**: specific

The summarization task was the same for both human and automatic summarizers: Given a DUC topic with granularity specification and a set of documents relevant to the topic, the summarization task was to create from the documents a brief, well-organized, fluent summary that answers the need for information expressed in the topic, at the specified level of granularity. The summary could be no longer than 250 words (whitespace-delimited tokens). Summaries over the size limit were truncated, and no bonus was given for creating a shorter summary. No specific formatting other than linear was allowed. The summary should include (in some form or other) all the information in the documents that contributed to meeting the information need.

Ten assessors produced a total of 9 human summaries for each of 20 topics, and 4 human summaries for each of the remaining 30 topics. The summarization task was a relatively difficult task, requiring about 5 hours to manually create each summary. Thus, there would be a real benefit to users if the task could be performed automatically.

## 3 Participants

There was much interest in the longer, question-focused summaries required in the DUC 2005 task. 31 participants submitted runs to the evaluation; they are identified by numeric Run IDs (2-32) in the remainder of this paper. We also developed a simple baseline system that returned the first 250 words of the most recent document for each topic (Run ID = 1). In addition to the automatic peers, there were 10 human peers, assigned alphabetic Run IDs, A-J.

Most system developers treated the summarization task as a passage retrieval task. Sentences were ranked according to relevance to the topic. The most relevant sentences were then selected for inclusion in the summary while minimizing redundancy within the summary, up to the maximum 250-word allowance. A significant minority of systems first decomposed the topic narrative into a set of simpler questions, and then extracted sentences to answer each subquestion. Systems differed in the approach taken to compute relevance and redundancy, using similarity metrics ranging from simple term frequency to semantic graph matching. In order to include more relevant information in the summary, systems attempted within-sentence compression by removing phrases such as parentheticals and relative clauses.

Many systems simply ignored the granularity specification. The systems that addressed granularity did so by preferring to extract sentences that contained proper names for topics with a "specific" granularity but not for topics with "general" granularity.

Cross-sentence dependencies had to be handled, including anaphora. Strategies for dealing with pronouns that occurred in relevant sentences included co-reference resolution, including the previous sentence for additional context, or simply excluding all sentences containing any pronouns.

Most systems made no attempt to reword the extracted sentences to improve the readability of the final summary. Although some systems grouped related sentences together to improve cohesion, the most common heuristic to improve readability was simply to order the extracted sentences by document date and position in the document. System 12 achieved high readability scores by choosing a single representative document and extracting sentences in the order of appearance in that document. This approach is similar to the baseline summarizer and produces summaries that are more fluent than those constructed from multiple documents.

## 4 Evaluation Results

Summaries were manually evaluated by 10 assessors. All summaries for a given topic were judged by a single assessor (who was usually the same as the topic developer). In all cases, the assessor was one of the summarizers for the topic. All summaries for the topic (including the one written by the assessor) were anonymously presented to the assessor, in a random order, and the ssessor judged each summary for readability and responsiveness to the topic, giving separate scores for responsiveness and each of 5 linguistic qualities. This allowed participants who could not work on optimizing all 6 manual scores, to focus on only the elements that they were interested in or had the resources to address.

No single score was reported that reflected a combination of readability and content. In previous years, responsiveness considered both the content and readability of the summary. While it tracked SEE coverage, responsiveness could not be seen as a direct measure of content due to possible effects of readability on the score. Because we needed an inexpensive manual measure of coverage, we revised the definition of responsiveness in 2005 so that it considered only the information content and not the readability of the summary, to the extent possible.

### 4.1 Evaluation of Readability

The readability of the summaries was assessed using five linguistic quality questions which measured qualities of the summary that *do not* involve comparison with a reference summary or DUC topic. The linguistic qualities measured were *Grammaticality, Non-redundancy, Referential clarity, Focus, and Structure and coherence.*

**Q1: Grammaticality** The summary should have no datelines, system-internal formatting, capitalization errors or obviously ungrammatical sentences (e.g., fragments, missing components) that make the text difficult to read.

**Q2: Non-redundancy** There should be no unnecessary repetition in the summary. Unnecessary repetition might take the form of whole sentences that are repeated, or repeated facts, or the repeated use of a noun or noun phrase (e.g., "Bill Clinton") when a pronoun ("he") would suffice.

**Q3: Referential clarity** It should be easy to identify who or what the pronouns and noun phrases in the summary are referring to. If a person or other entity is mentioned, it should be clear what their role in the story is. So, a reference would be unclear if an entity is referenced but its identity or relation to the story remains unclear.

**Q4: Focus** The summary should have a focus; sentences should only contain information that is related to the rest of the summary.

**Q5: Structure and Coherence** The summary should be well-structured and well-organized. The summary should not just be a heap of related information, but should build from sentence to sentence to a coherent body of information about a topic.

Each linguistic quality question was assessed on a five-point scale:

1. Very Poor
2. Poor
3. Barely Acceptable
4. Good
5. Very Good

Table 1 shows the distribution of the scores across all the summaries, broken down by the type of summarizer (Human, Baseline, or Participants). All summarizers generally performed well on the first two linguistic qualities. The high scores on non-redundancy show that most participants have

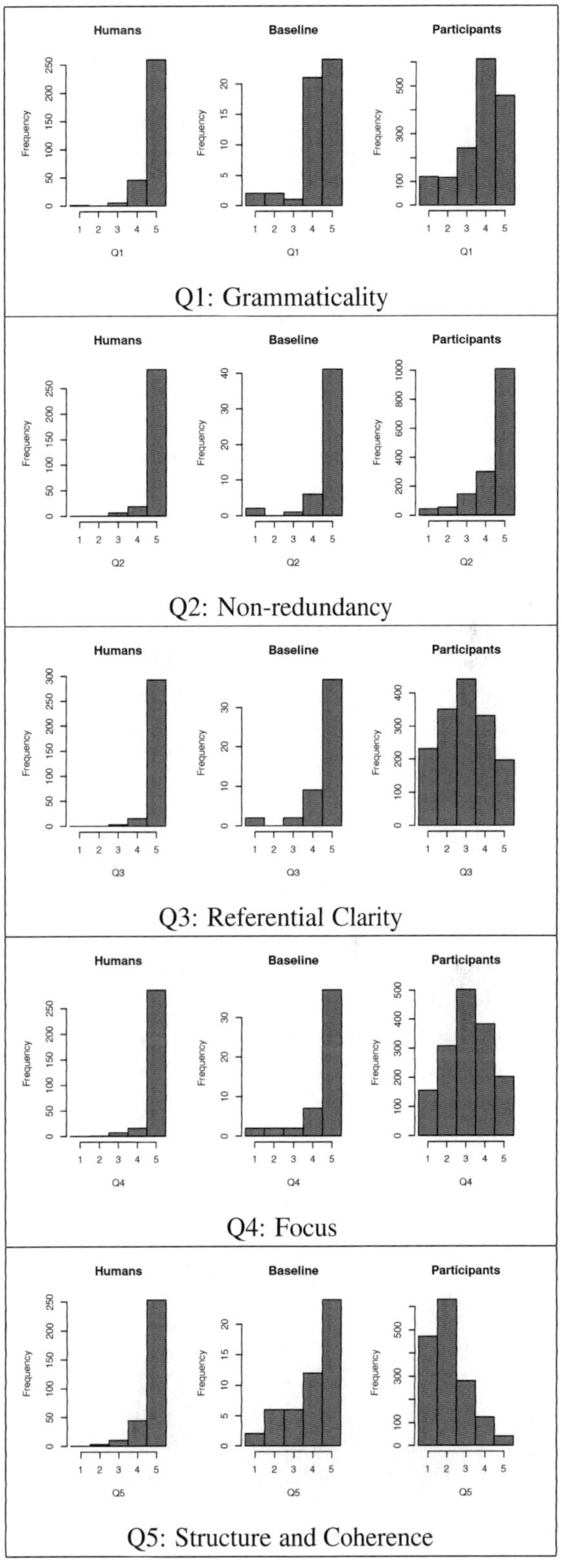


Table 1: Frequency of scores for each linguistic quality, broken down by source of summary (Humans, Baseline, Participants).

successfully achieved this capability. Humans and the baseline system also scored well on the last 3 linguistic qualities. The multi-document summarization systems submitted by participants, on the other hand, still struggle with referential clarity and focus, and perform very poorly on structure and coherence.

#### 4.1.1 Comparison by system

For each linguistic quality question, we performed a multiple comparison test between the scores of all peers using Tukey's honestly significant difference criterion. A multiple comparison test between all human and automatic peers was performed using the Kruskall-Wallis test, to see how the individual automatic peers performed relative to human peers. For grammaticality, the best human summarizer is significantly better than 28 of the 32 systems; the worst human summarizer is better than 8 systems. For non-redundancy, the two best humans are significantly better than 6 systems, and the two worst humans are not significantly different from any system. For referential clarity, all humans are significantly better than all but 2 automatic peers (baseline and System 12). For focus, the best human is significantly better than all automatic peers except the baseline; all other humans are significantly better than all automatic peers except the baseline and System 12. For structure and coherence, the two best humans are significantly better than 31 systems (all automatic peers except the baseline); all humans are better than 30 of the automatic peers (all automatic peers except baseline and System 12).

### 4.2 Evaluation of Content

We performed manual pseudo-extrinsic evaluation of peer summaries in the form of assessment of responsiveness. Responsiveness is different from SEE coverage in that it does not compare a peer summary against a single reference; however, responsiveness tracked SEE coverage in DUC 2003 and 2004, and was used to provide a coarse-grained measure of content in 2005. We also computed ROUGE scores as was done in DUC 2004.

#### 4.2.1 Responsiveness

Assessors assigned a raw responsiveness score to each summary. The score provides a coarse ranking of the summaries for each topic, according to the amount of information in the summary that helps to satisfy the information need expressed in the topic statement, at the level of granularity requested in the user profile. The score was an integer between 1 and 5, with 1 being least responsive and 5 being most responsive. For a given topic, some summary was required to receive each of the five possible scores, but no distribution was specified for how many summaries had to receive each score. The number of human summaries scored per topic also varied. Therefore, raw responsiveness scores should not be directly added and compared across topics. Assigning responsiveness scores can be seen as a clustering task in which peers are partitioned into exactly 5 clusters, where members of a cluster are more similar to each other in quality.

| RunID | | | | | | | |
|---|---|---|---|---|---|---|---|
| 10 | A | | | | | | |
| 5 | A | | | | | | |
| 4 | A | B | | | | | |
| 15 | A | B | C | | | | |
| 29 | A | B | C | D | | | |
| 11 | A | B | C | D | | | |
| 17 | A | B | C | D | | | |
| 8 | A | B | C | D | | | |
| 7 | A | B | C | D | E | | |
| 14 | A | B | C | D | E | | |
| 6 | A | B | C | D | E | | |
| 28 | A | B | C | D | E | F | |
| 21 | A | B | C | D | E | F | |
| 19 | A | B | C | D | E | F | |
| 24 | A | B | C | D | E | F | |
| 9 | A | B | C | D | E | F | |
| 16 | A | B | C | D | E | F | |
| 32 | A | B | C | D | E | F | |
| 12 | A | B | C | D | E | F | |
| 25 | A | B | C | D | E | F | |
| 18 | A | B | C | D | E | F | |
| 27 | A | B | C | D | E | F | |
| 20 | A | B | C | D | E | F | |
| 3 | A | B | C | D | E | F | |
| 2 | | B | C | D | E | F | |
| 13 | | | C | D | E | F | |
| 30 | | | | D | E | F | |
| 22 | | | | | E | F | |
| 1 | | | | | E | F | |
| 26 | | | | | | F | |
| 31 | | | | | | F | G |
| 23 | | | | | | | G |

Table 2: Multiple comparison of systems based on Friedman's test on responsiveness

For each topic, we computed the scaled responsiveness score for each summary, such that the sum of the scaled responsiveness score is proportional to the number of summaries for the topic. The scaled responsiveness is the rank of the summary based on the raw responsiveness score. We computed the average scaled responsiveness score of each summarizer across all topics. Since the number of human summaries varied across topics, we also computed the average scaled responsiveness score of only the automatic summaries (ignoring the human summaries in scaling responsiveness).

Table 2 shows the results of a multiple comparison of scaled responsiveness of the automatic peers using Tukey's honestly significant criterion and Friedman's test, with the best peers on top; peers not sharing a common letter are significantly different at the 95.5% confidence level. None of the automatic peers performed significantly better than the majority of the remaining peers, and only eight of the automatic peers performed significantly better than the simple baseline. In multiple comparison of all peers using the Kruskal-Wallis test, all human peers were significantly better than all the automatic peers.

#### 4.2.2 ROUGE

We computed two ROUGE scores: ROUGE-2 and ROUGE-SU4 recall, both with stemming and implementing jackknifing for each $[peer, topic]$ pair so that human and automatic peers could be compared. Since the number of ROUGE evaluations per topic varied depending on the number of reference summaries, we computed a macro-average of each score for each peer, where the macro-average score is the mean over all topics of the mean per-topic score for the peer.

Unlike responsiveness and linguistic quality scores, which are ordinal data and are best suited for non-parametric analyses, ROUGE scores, can be measured on an interval scale and are suitable for parametric analysis. Analysis of variance showed significant effects from peer and topic ($p = 0$ for each factor) for both ROUGE-2 and ROUGE-SU4 recall. To see which peers were different, a multiple comparison of population marginal means (PMM) was performed for each type of ROUGE score. The population marginal means remove any effect of an unbalanced design (since not all human peers created summaries for all topics) by fixing the values of the "peer" factor, and averaging out the effects of the "topic" factor as if each factor combination occurred the same number of times.

Table 3 shows multiple comparison of all peers based on ANOVA of ROUGE-2 recall (ROUGE-SU4 shows similar results). ROUGE-2 and ROUGE-SU4 both distinguish human peers from automatic ones. The difference in the ROUGE-2

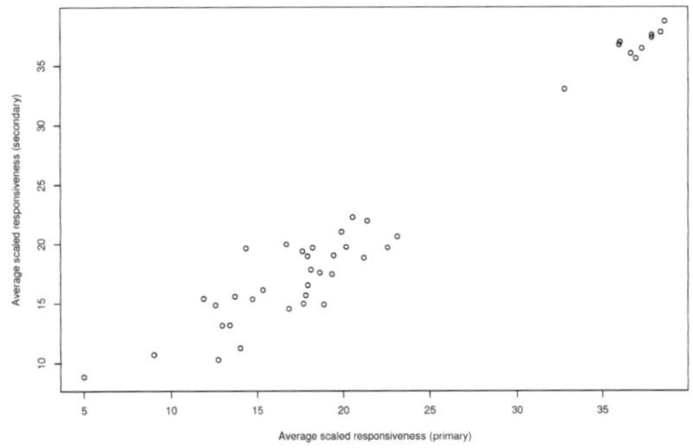


Figure 1: Primary vs. secondary average scaled responsiveness

score of the best system and worst human is not considered significant (possibly due to the very conservative nature of the multiple comparison test) but is still relatively large. On the other hand, ANOVA of ROUGE-2 found more significant differences between the automatic peers than did Friedman's test of responsiveness.

### 4.3 Correlation

A metric must produce stable rankings of systems in the face of human variation. Intrinsic measures like ROUGE rely on multiple model summaries to take into account human variation (although Pyramids add another level of human variation in the manual pyramid and peer annotation). For a metric like responsiveness, which does not depend on comparison of peer summaries against a model or set of model summaries, it is appropriate to consider the stability of the measure across different assessors.

A secondary assessment was done on responsiveness for the 20 topics that had 9 summaries each. The secondary assessor had written a summary for the topic but was generally not the same person who developed the topic. As seen in Figure 1, average scaled responsiveness scores from the two sets of assessments (averaged over the 20 topics) track each other very well. The human summaries are clustered on the upper right side of the graph, while the automatic summaries form a second cluster on the lower left side.

The actual responsiveness scores for each system and each topic do vary between assessors, but this variation in human judgment is smoothed out by averaging over multiple topics. Table 4 shows that the correlation between the primary and sec-

| RunID | PMM of R2 | | | | | | | | | | | | | |
|---|---|---|---|---|---|---|---|---|---|---|---|---|---|---|
| C | 0.1172 | A | | | | | | | | | | | | |
| A | 0.1156 | A | B | | | | | | | | | | | |
| I | 0.1023 | A | B | C | | | | | | | | | | |
| B | 0.1014 | A | B | C | | | | | | | | | | |
| J | 0.1012 | A | B | C | | | | | | | | | | |
| E | 0.1009 | A | B | C | | | | | | | | | | |
| D | 0.0986 | A | B | C | | | | | | | | | | |
| G | 0.0970 | | B | C | | | | | | | | | | |
| F | 0.0947 | | | C | | | | | | | | | | |
| H | 0.0897 | | | C | D | | | | | | | | | |
| 15 | 0.0725 | | | | D | E | | | | | | | | |
| 17 | 0.0717 | | | | | E | | | | | | | | |
| 10 | 0.0698 | | | | | E | F | | | | | | | |
| 8 | 0.0696 | | | | | E | F | | | | | | | |
| 4 | 0.0686 | | | | | E | F | G | | | | | | |
| 5 | 0.0675 | | | | | E | F | G | | | | | | |
| 11 | 0.0643 | | | | | E | F | G | H | | | | | |
| 14 | 0.0635 | | | | | E | F | G | H | I | | | | |
| 16 | 0.0633 | | | | | E | F | G | H | I | | | | |
| 19 | 0.0632 | | | | | E | F | G | H | I | | | | |
| 7 | 0.0628 | | | | | E | F | G | H | I | J | | | |
| 9 | 0.0625 | | | | | E | F | G | H | I | J | | | |
| 29 | 0.0609 | | | | | E | F | G | H | I | J | K | | |
| 25 | 0.0609 | | | | | E | F | G | H | I | J | K | | |
| 6 | 0.0609 | | | | | E | F | G | H | I | J | K | | |
| 24 | 0.0597 | | | | | E | F | G | H | I | J | K | | |
| 28 | 0.0594 | | | | | E | F | G | H | I | J | K | | |
| 3 | 0.0594 | | | | | E | F | G | H | I | J | K | | |
| 21 | 0.0573 | | | | | E | F | G | H | I | J | K | | |
| 12 | 0.0563 | | | | | | F | G | H | I | J | K | | |
| 18 | 0.0553 | | | | | | F | G | H | I | J | K | L | |
| 26 | 0.0547 | | | | | | F | G | H | I | J | K | L | |
| 27 | 0.0546 | | | | | | F | G | H | I | J | K | L | |
| 32 | 0.0534 | | | | | | | G | H | I | J | K | L | |
| 20 | 0.0515 | | | | | | | | H | I | J | K | L | |
| 13 | 0.0497 | | | | | | | | H | I | J | K | L | |
| 30 | 0.0496 | | | | | | | | H | I | J | K | L | |
| 31 | 0.0487 | | | | | | | | | I | J | K | L | |
| 2 | 0.0478 | | | | | | | | | | J | K | L | |
| 22 | 0.0462 | | | | | | | | | | | K | L | |
| 1 | 0.0403 | | | | | | | | | | | | L | M |
| 23 | 0.0256 | | | | | | | | | | | | | M |

Table 3: Multiple comparison of all peers based on ANOVA of ROUGE-2 recall

| | Spearman | Pearson |
|---|---|---|
| All peers | 0.900 | 0.976 [0.960, 1.000] |
| Auto peers | 0.775 | 0.822 [0.695, 1.000] |

Table 4: Correlation between primary and secondary average scaled responsiveness (20 topics), with 95% confidence intervals for Pearson's $r$.

ondary average scaled responsiveness scores is respectable despite the low number of topics. The correlation suggests that responsiveness would give a stable ranking of the systems when averaged over the entire set of 50 topics.

Table 5 shows that there is high correlation between macro-average ROUGE scores (intrinsic measures) and average scaled responsiveness (a pseudo-extrinisic measure). The correlation is high even when the human summaries are ignored.

| Metric | Spearman | Pearson |
|---|---|---|
| ROUGE-2 (all) | 0.951 | 0.972 [0.953, 1.000] |
| ROUGE-SU4 (all) | 0.942 | 0.958 [0.930, 1.000] |
| ROUGE-2 (auto) | 0.901 | 0.928 [0.872, 1.000] |
| ROUGE-SU4 (auto) | 0.872 | 0.919 [0.855, 1.000] |

Table 5: Correlation between average scaled responsiveness and macro-average ROUGE recall over all topics and either all peers or only automatic peers.

## 5 Conclusion

The DUC 2005 task was to summarize the answer to a complex question, as found in a set of documents. The evaluation showed that only the top systems are able to extract sentences whose information content is more responsive to the question than a simple baseline. Additionally, systems require much additional work to produce coherent, well-structured text, which is apparent in the longer summary sizes of DUC 2005. On the other hand, systems do well on non-redundancy, since text summarization has historically been formulated as a text compression task. Since DUC 2005 is the first time question-focused summarization has been evaluated on a large-scale, we have repeated the task in 2006, with some modifications.

We eliminated the "granularity" specification in DUC 2006. Assessors had appreciated the theory behind the granularity specification, but found that the size limit for the summaries was a much bigger factor in determining what information to include; some "specific" summaries ended up being very general given the large amount of information and limited space allowed. From a human perspective, the actual granularity of the resulting summary mostly fell out naturally from the topic question and the content that was available in the source documents.

The definition of responsiveness scores was meant to yield a coarse ranking of the peer summaries into 5 ordered clusters. However, assessors found it difficult to form these 5 clusters because of the large number (36+) of summaries that needed to be compared with one another, and the impression that many sets of human and automatic summaries could not be separated into as many as 5 groups. We therefore changed the scoring of responsiveness in 2006 so that it is based on the same scale as the linguistic quality questions; this may reduce the discriminative power of the responsiveness measure but should produce scores that more accurately reflect the true differences between summaries.

## References


Enrique Amigo, Julio Gonzalo, Victor Peinado, Anselmo Penas, and Felisa Verdejo. 2004. An empirical study of information synthesis tasks. In *Proceedings of the 42nd Annual Meeting of the Association for Computational Linguistics*, pages 207–214, Barcelona, Spain.

Donna Harman and Paul Over. 2004. The effects of human variation in duc summarization evaluation. In *Proceedings of the ACL-04 Workshop: Text Summarization Branches Out*, pages 10–17, Barcelona, Spain.

Eduard Hovy, Chin-Yew Lin, and Liang Zhou. 2005. Evaluating duc 2005 using basic elements. In *Proceedings of the Fifth Document Understanding Conference (DUC)*, Vancouver, Canada.

Chin-Yew Lin. 2004. Rouge: A package for automatic evaluation of summaries. In *Proceedings of the ACL-04 Workshop: Text Summarization Branches Out*, pages 74–81, Barcelona, Spain.

Rebecca J. Passonneau, Ani Nenkova, Kathleen McKeown, and Sergey Sigelman. 2005. Applying the pyramid method in duc 2005. In *Proceedings of the Fifth Document Understanding Conference (DUC)*, Vancouver, Canada.

Ellen M. Voorhees and Chris Buckley. 2002. The effect of topic set size on retrieval experiment error. In *Proceedings of the 25th Annual International ACM SIGIR Conference on Research and Development in Information Retrieval*, pages 316–323, Tampere, Finland, August.

# Author Index